Timing
Is
Everything

How to recognize, predict and capitalize on the seven stages all trends experience.

Dr. Amy Vanderbilt

Trend Factor Press

Published by Trend Factor Press
a division of Vanderbilt Consulting LLC
Purcellville, Virginia USA
www.TrendFactorPress.com

ISBN - 13: 978-0-9818669-9-4
ISBN - 10: 0-9818669-9-9

First Edition

Printed in the United States of America

Many thanks to Clarissa Chiu and Carole Wirszyla of the TrendPOV.com team for research and contributions to this work. This would not have happened without you!

Disclaimer

Dr. Amy Vanderbilt and associated personnel at TrendPOV.com and Vanderbilt Consulting do not give investment advice online or in this book. They are not registered investment advisors. The information in this book and online are general in nature and intended to inform and enlighten. Trend stages are one piece of information in a larger set of data that you should consider before investing your time, effort and money in anything. Dr. Vanderbilt and the team at TrendPOV.com and Vanderbilt consulting discourage you from using trend stages as the only piece of information in your decision making. All investment contains risk. Please seek professional advice before investing.

About The Author

Business and Technology Strategist, Senior Fellow of the Potomac Institute and a former DARPA program manager, Dr. Vanderbilt brings blunt honesty and a unique ability to recognize to the technologies and businesses poised for growth, and what it will take to get them to the next level.

Dr. Amy Vanderbilt is the Founder and Chief Strategist at TrendPOV.com, next generation social omni-media that over one MILLION executives call GPS for your business strategy. She consults to venture capital and private equity firms on investment strategy, scouting, due diligence, portfolio management and portfolio incubation. To date, she has reviewed more than 1200 concepts for funding and application in numerous innovative ways, and more than 600 companies for their growth and innovative potential.

She is an award winning author and keynote speaker. *Timing is Everything* is her sixth book in publication.

She holds a PhD in Mathematics focused on Nonmonotonic Reasoning and a passion for early STEM education, education technology and education policy.

Her technical expertise, as a matter of design, now encompasses a broad range of application areas including: Wearable Displays, Augmented Reality, Network Analysis, Information Visualization, Video Analysis, New Media, Space Based Systems, Virtual Worlds, Sensor Systems, Nano-technology, Online Intelligence, Persistent Surveillance, Cyber Defense/Attack, and Green Energy.

Learn more and contact Dr. Vanderbilt at DrAmyVanderbilt.com.

Contents

Introduction 17

    How This Book is Organized   18

    Trend Data   19

Timing is Everything   21

Recognizing a Trend   25

Understanding How Trends Start, Grow and Change   37

    Stage 1 - First Try   37

        Overview   37

        Example - Zip Car   38

        Conclusions 39

    Stage 2 - Getting Real 40

        Overview   40

        Example - Biofuel   41

        Example - Influence Marketing   42

Example - Social Gaming 43

Example - Multi-Generational Workforce 44

Example - Social Network Search 45

Example: Under The Influence - Understanding The Stage Two Trend of Influence Marketing 46

Conclusions 53

Stage 3 - First Utility 55

Overview 55

Example - Mobile Security 56

Example - Crowdsourcing 56

Example: Young and In Charge - Managing The Stage Three Trend Of Generational Reversal 57

Example: The Smug And The Restless - Understanding Mobile Security As A Stage Three Trend 65

Conclusions 73

Stage 4 - Limitations 74

Overview   74

Example - Crowdfunding   75

Example - Augmented Reality   76

Example - Voice Recognition   77

Example - Virtual Teams   78

Example: Crowdfunding - Tracking This Stage Four Trend   79

Example: Talking Back - Understanding The Stage Four Trend Of Voice Based Systems   86

Conclusions 93

Stage 5 - Second Utility94

Overview   94

Example: Cyber Warfare - Anticipating Setbacks For This Stage Five Trend 95

Conclusions 103

Stage 6 - The Competitive Tidal Wave   104

Overview   104

Example - Visualization Software 105

Example - Tablets   106

Example - Terrorism 107

Example - Business Incubators   109

Example - Facebook   109

Example: Data Visualization - Tracking This Stage Six Trend   110

Example: Private Incubators - Acting on This Stage Six Trend   117

Conclusions 125

Stage 7 - Longevity   126

Overview   126

Example - Sustainability   126

Example - Chocolate   127

Example - Business Advisors   128

Example - Social Media   128

Example - Digital Marketing   129

Example - Samsung, Apple and LinkedIn   130

Example: Google - Learning From This Stage Seven Supertrend   132

Conclusions 140

Making Your Move 141

Convergence and Divergence   147

Example: Your Company IS The Product - Converging Trends Affecting The Design of Your Business (2012)   151

Example: Living in the Swarm—Converging Trends Redefining the Marketplace (2011)   155

Example: Striking the Balance - Converging Trends Driving Global Networks with Local Implications (2011)   162

Example: Putting On The Breaks - How The Simplicity Backlash May Slow Efforts To Reach Your Team (2011)   170

Example: Rule of All - Converging Trends Driving Your Digital Strategies (2011) 177

Example: All that SAAS - Converging Trends Driven By This Rapidly Evolving Model (2010)   185

Example: Your New Best Friend - Converging Trends Making Governments A Necessary Partner (2010)   192

Example: Individual Talent - Converging Trends Driving Your Workforce Strategies (2010)   199

Example: Driven Digital - Converging Trends Driving The Next Payment Method (2010)   206

Advanced Concepts   213

The Tea Leaves Are Hidden   213

Example - Mobile Learning 213

A Product Ahead Of Its Time   214

Trends, Trends Everywhere   217

Seeing Trends Everywhere? Excellent! Welcome to My World. 217

Angel and Venture Investing   218

Product Development   219

Innovative Uses 220

Career Moves: Leaving Industries and
Companies; and Entering New Ones 221

Conclusions   223

Resources   225

Introduction

Timing Is Everything is the culmination of years upon years of trend watching and a bit of geeky math obsession. Having run Trend POV for several years I had grown its audience of C-suite executives to over one million by tracking trends and predicting what would happen next. I was often asked how i chose which trend to follow, how i know what to do about each trend and how i seem to have an uncanny way of knowing when to act. What information do I take in? What am I looking for? And what is it about a trend that says to me: this one is worth talking about and acting on.

When I charted out all the answers to these questions, what I saw was the effective and efficient system for recognizing and acting on trends that had been stored away in my head all this time. As pleased as I was to see there was a repeatable method to my madness, I thought it should be shared so that everyone can use it.

How This Book is Organized

This book is organized as a learning resource. It begins with an overview of why trends evolve through seven distinct stages and what each stage entails. We proceed through recognizing a trend versus a fad. Moving on, we discuss the details of each stage and how trend start, grow and change over time. The juicy part comes next as we discuss what to do at each stage in the section "Making Your Move."

No book on this topic would be complete without delving into more advanced concepts such as what happens when trends converge and diverge, what to do when your product is ahead of its time, or when the tea leaves are hidden and hard to read.

Eventually, you will, as I do, see trend everywhere in your industry and business. That's great! We discuss how to cope with that realization and how to (call it selfish!), use all of this new knowledge in your own personal career and business efforts.

This book should be used to learn, and as a reference. It is NOT intended as a stock investment strategy... certainly not by itself. It is a guide to one important piece of the puzzle when determining whether to invest your time, effort and possibly money into a business, industry or concept.

Trend Data

The graphs seen throughout the book are representations of public interest (a combination of technology, momentum and utility). In real life, I recommend using Google Trends data. Here, we have abstracted this type of search and news frequency data to help focus on the general shape of the data as we learn to recognize each trend stage.

Timing is Everything

The large majority of trends go through seven distinct phases or stages. Making the right move in each stage is the key to creating advantage for yourself and your business.

Hindsight is 20/20. We've all looked back and wish we acted on opportunities to be the part of something big. Either by investment, effort, or being a player in the product space. How many wished they had gotten involved, as an investor, as an employee, as an advisor, and more with the likes of Apple or Google? How many wish they had made an earlier start on social media, or mobile efforts? Great opportunities are easy to see in hindsight but hard to see as they are approaching and even as they are happening.

Making the right move at the right time is critical. Venture investors make a living off predicting which company, concept and industry is the next big thing. They each have a secret sauce formula. One thing they know is that there are lots of factors that make an opportunity the one to take. The people involved, the idea, the industry and the market are all important factors. Then there is something more... the issue of whether now is the time.

Trend stages are my secret sauce. When asked to sit on a board, consult, endorse, or otherwise put forth my own time, money and effort, I take a look at the people, ideas, industry, and most importantly, at the trend stage. Trend stages are important when trying to decide WHEN. When to invest time, money or effort in a company, when to launch a product, when to use a technology for a particular purpose, and more.

Your foresight doesn't have to be 50/50.Too many decisions come down to a coin toss, even when all the other factors line up. Gut instinct is your next best thing, and this is not to suggest you ignore your gut. You should never ignore that. But what if you could have something a bit more concrete to guide you?

The overwhelming majority of trends follow the same path of launch, growth and change. The development of each can be tracked, and to a great extent, anticipated.

Trends evolve through seven distinct stages of growth and decline. These stages look a lot like

Elliot Waves from the world of finance theory and trading. It is not surprising as Elliot Waves are just a byproduct of natural human chaos. That chaos shows itself just as readily in the world of business trends as it does in the stock market.

In the following picture, we show where many of today's trends are along these seven stages. This is current as of the date of this book. You can be certain that they will move. The key is in understanding the stages and learning how to predict what comes next.

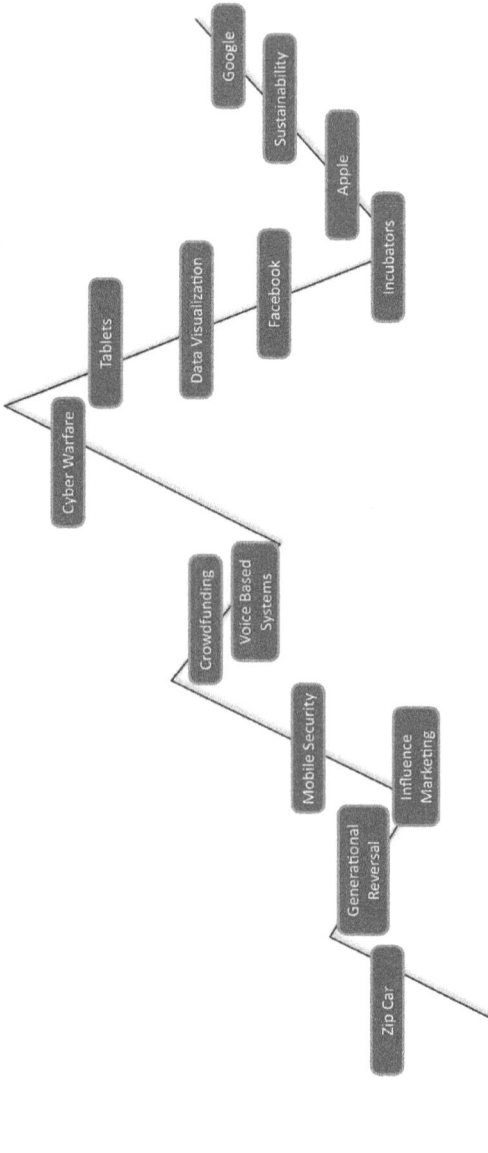

Trend Stage Map (As Of September 2013)

Google
Sustainability
Apple
Incubators
Facebook
Data Visualization
Tablets
Cyber Warfare
Crowdfunding
Voice Based Systems
Mobile Security
Influence Marketing
Generational Reversal
Zip Car

Recognizing a Trend

So, what is a trend? A business trend is when something about the business environment is changing. It could be just one aspect that is evolving or something entirely new. It could affect your operations, talent and workforce, global ambitions, business model, payment systems, supply chain or other critical aspects of your business.

Trends are not fads. Trends result in waves of interest for years to decades and then typically evolve into or spawn other trends. For example, mobile payment systems, 3D printing, and influence marketing are all trends in various stages.

Augmented reality, for example, is a trend in stage four. Below is it's trend data. You can see in the graph how the general interest in the subject of augmented reality is largely flat for a while, then increases sharply, takes a break, increases again, then appears to be in a bit of a downturn.

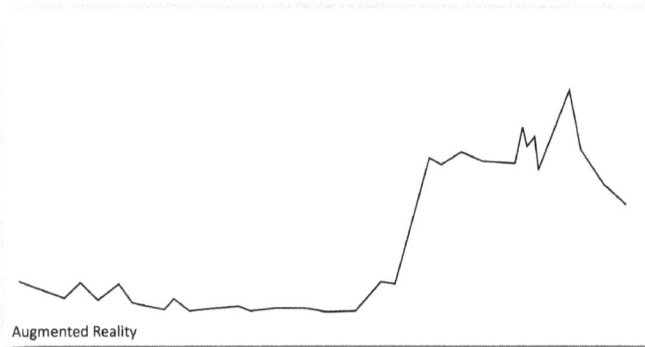

Augmented Reality

Virtual teams, seen below, is another example of a trend. This trend is also in stage four. Trends, in general, are sustained.

Virtual Teams

Fads in contrast are fun, short term, cultural memes. If it is cute and fun but largely useless, its a fad, not a trend. Silly Bandz, Pet Rocks and Justin Beiber, for example, are all fads.

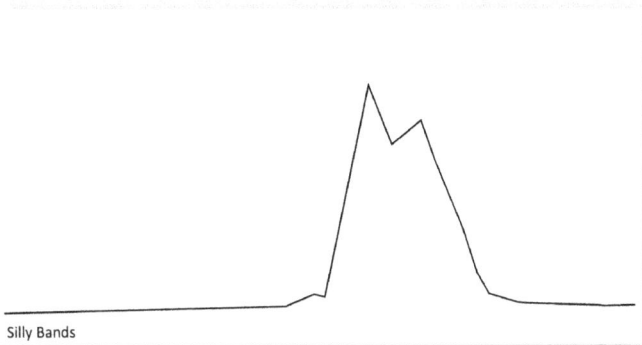

Silly Bands

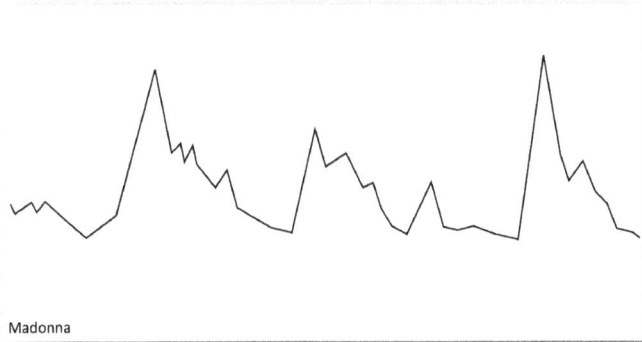

Madonna

Notice the spikes interest that are not sustained. That doesn't mean you cannot make money from them. In fact, consider Madonna who has patented techniques for renewing her fad status that have produced more revenue than most businesses ever hope.

Trends however, will produce revenue and other returns with more stability and predictability, than fads. Trends move forward, not backwards.

All trends start out the same way. Hype builds over potential prototypes and ideas. Technology is almost there. Social permission is close at hand. It has lots of potential IF it can get out of the gate.

All trends are MUTs... Momentum, Utility and Technology must all be in place to make them happen, and to push them to the next stage.

Momentum is about public interest. A business must have permission from its customers to exist, and grow. So must an industry. Momentum is about hype, press, word of mouth, and general excitement. Momentum is also about the creative force in the form of people to drive the trend forward.

A trend must eventually have at least two utilities. The first must have immediate return on investment such as marketing. The second can indulge in a bit longer term returns such as productivity, business intelligence, and other operations or workforce related effects. A given trend may have dozens to hundreds of utilities. In fact, the more the better. But presenting them all at the same time too early in a trend's evolution will overwhelm users and have you starting over at square one.

The technology must be ready and available. A bit of required development is fine, but if too great a distance exists between the technology available and the technology required to make it happen, the trend will stall and possibly fail.

The opportunity must exist for the technology, momentum, and utility to all come together in a simple and powerful way. If it does, you have a trend in the making. That trend will then proceed through seven distinct stages: first try, getting real, first utility, limitations, second utility, the competitive tidal wave, and at last longevity.

To take advantage of trend stages, you must first understanding how trends start, grow and change. Let's take a quick look as each stage. We will go more in depth in a later section of the book.

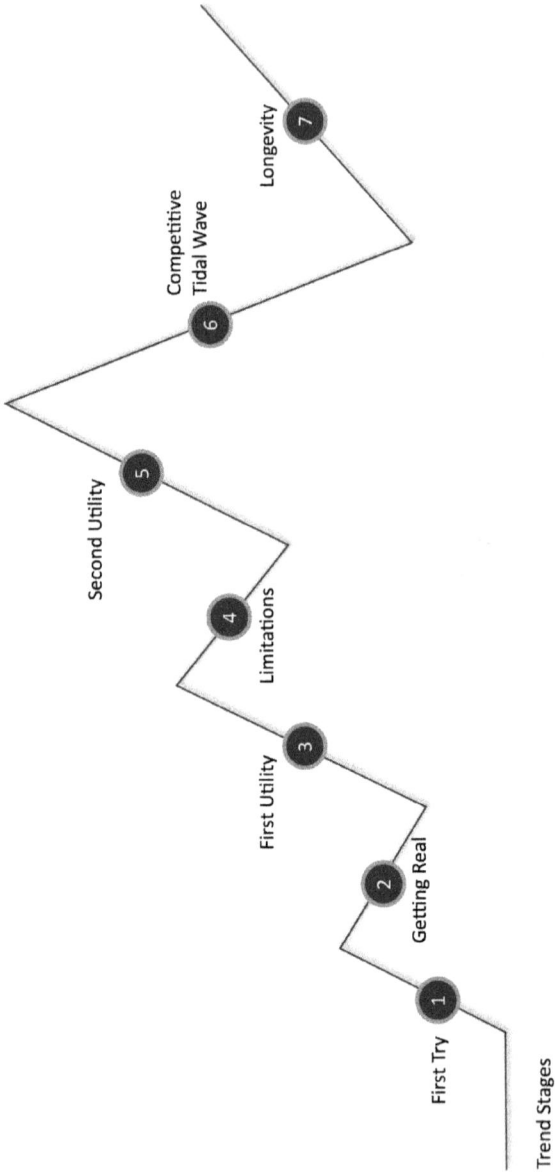

Trend Stages

1 — First Try
2 — Getting Real
3 — First Utility
4 — Limitations
5 — Second Utility
6 — Competitive Tidal Wave
7 — Longevity

Stage 1, First Try, is when the first prototypes of the technology, business model, industry, service, etc are attempted. There are sparks of public interest, hype in the press, and discussion online and around the water coolers. A few brave investors will get involved (very high risk). The trend has not yet found its first real utility in this stage; instead, it is just trying some things out. As a result, first tries tend to move into stage two when their lack of polish is no longer cute.

Stage 2, Getting Real, is when public interest pulls back from this trend. That bit of experimentation in stage one was fun, but we have real businesses to run here. Momentum wanes, technology may stall out or have trouble moving forward, and the first real utility is still forming. Towards the end of this stage, however, once a real first utility is discovered, this trend will take off.

Stage 3, First Utility, is where we see the first real, polished and tested products, services, and monetization of a trend. Momentum picks up significantly as hype, excitement and discussion about this new useful thing for immediate return on investment ripples through the business world. We are a fickle bunch, however, and soon enough we are complacent and spoiled. The first utility is just not enough anymore, and social permission drops off as the public complains about how limited this trend really is.

Stage 4, Limitations, is where businesses acting on this trend must get clever. Interest, and possibly revenues at this stage have pulled back yet again. Momentum stalls as headlines suggest that maybe this trend is past its peak and not the great thing we all thought it might be. At this stage, finding the second real utility is key.

Stage 5, Second Utility, is where we see the largest amount of solid business growth for any given trend. Momentum picks back up as headlines and individuals return to their original excitement. Technology is well in hand to make it happen, and businesses acting on this trend seem to really be solidifying their place in the world. Enter the competition... and plenty of it.

Stage 6, The Competitive Tidal Wave, is where we see giants fall (or so it would seem). The rush of competition threatens to commoditize the offering. Customers, once again, become complacent and spoiled and complain about the little things that could be improved. Often in this stage, the word on the street will sound like, "It would be perfect, if they would only..." The competition is acting on those "if onlys." The future of efforts for this trend seems really uncertain, as it suffers the largest setback of its existence. At this stage, the trend and those involved with it, must figure out what it will look like long term. They must retool for longevity. If they can, stage 7 will be wonderful, indeed.

Stage 7, Longevity, is where trends, and the businesses involved with them, achieve long term success. In this stage, company stability and the careers they have fostered seem very solid indeed. And at last, they are. In this stage, the trend is now here to stay and will likely begin to spawn new trends that will start the cycle all over again.

Not all trends will make it through all seven stages. If the technology is not in place, a trend can stall out for years before having to restart back at stage one. If the utility is never found, it will die in stage two and be marked a fad. Every stage of each trend is fraught with peril. Each pullback stage is one where management and investment decisions will launch this trend, and the businesses who love it, into the next stage, or doom them to failure.

They key is knowing what move to make when. Understanding the stages, is the first step.

Critical Points

- Trends go through seven distinct stages. These stages are largely predictable.

- Making the right move at the right trend stage is key. Investment, careers moves, product launches and more should all be timed correctly.

- Trend stages make and break companies and careers. Making a move at the wrong time can mean the end of your company, your career in that industry, and your reputation.

- Check the trend stage before investing time, effort or money. It is just one piece of critical information, but an important one.

- Lastly, understanding trend stages is a powerful tool, simply because it informs your timing.

Dr. Amy Vanderbilt

Understanding How Trends Start, Grow and Change

Stage 1 - First Try

Overview

Stage 1, First Try, is when the first prototypes of the technology, business model, industry, service, etc are attempted. It is the first incarnations of the trend, and the first time most people ever consider its existence. It is an exciting time, for certain, and a time of great risk.

There are sparks of public interest, hype in the press, and discussion online and around the water coolers. A few brave investors will get involved (very high risk). Startup junkies will launch a new business around it. The momentum is real and significant enough to give the social permission needed to experiment with what this trend might be good for.

The trend has not yet found its first real utility in this stage; instead, it is just trying some things out.

There tends to be a shotgun pattern of businesses offering up various uses of this trend. The key will be in which utility directly relates to the bottom line of their customers, as that is the utility that tends to survive and push the trend ahead.

The technology in Stage One is not always complete. It is, however, complete enough that a little more development is all it takes to really launch this trend (and its associated businesses) into real growth.

Example - Zip Car

Zip Car

Zip Car is a great example of a business capitalizing on a trend in stage one. The concept of renting a car for just a few hours is a trend indeed. When Zip Car, and similar companies, first started out, the technology to make that happen was not completely there. They had to develop some methodologies and some software, and even a bit of hardware. The momentum was there and the press liked the idea enough to cover it quite a bit. Many concepts of the short term rental appeared: cars, bikes, even boats. Many of these concepts took off. At the time of writing, Zip Car was solidly in stage one; and enjoying all the excitement that comes with it, including funding, press coverage, and the thrill of the startup with great potential.

Conclusions

Stage one is a dangerous time for any trend. It has all the potential in the world, and all the risk as well. Momentum is there, utility is undefined as prototypes try lots of new possible uses, and the technology is not completely smooth and finished. As a result, first tries tend to move into stage two when their lack of polish and focus is no longer cute.

Stage 2 - Getting Real

Overview

Stage 2, Getting Real, is when public interest pulls back from the trend. That bit of experimentation in stage one was fun, but we have real businesses to run here. It would seem as if the trend was just a fad, and its time is over.

Momentum wanes. The press starts to ignore the trend as old news. Customers, frustrated with the buggy nature of stage one offerings take a break from buying. It is a hard time for businesses involved in these trends and a wake up call that the time for real action has come.

The first real utility is still forming. In stage one, there were so many possible utilities that people became overwhelmed. The first real use of the trend is in there somewhere but the public has not seriously latched on.

Technology in this stage may stall out or have trouble moving forward. If the buggy nature of the first prototypes cannot be resolved, customers may not return. This is a dangerous stage where trends can die off and become just another fad. Most, however, continue on.

Example - Biofuel

Biofuel was a hot topic. WAS, being the operative word. We don't hear as much about it anymore; mostly because the first biofuels were less than perfect, there were issues with the process to create it, and nobody could quite figure out who would really get the most use from it. Would it be transportation companies? Individuals? Militaries? For what vehicles exactly? It was all a little scattered and confused.

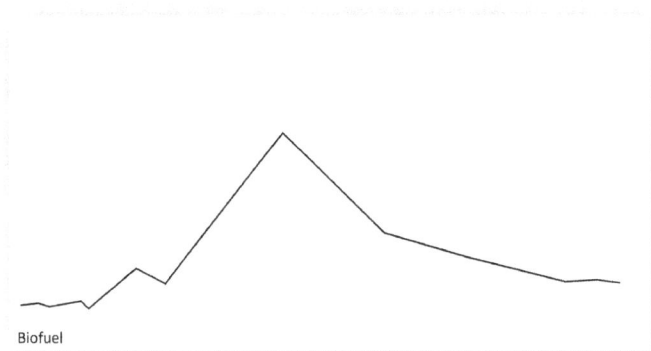

Biofuel

Biofuels, however, are not a fad. They are a trend in stage two. Notice the decline in their graph. But notice that the decline is not enough to take this trend all the way back down to its pre-stage one levels. There is sustainment here for the sustainment-oriented trend! That little bit of sustainment in momentum and overall interest is all it takes. This trend will indeed reach stage three at some point.

Example - Influence Marketing

Influence Marketing

Influence marketing looks like it might be in stage three. As of the time of writing, I am keeping it in stage two, because it has not escaped stage two enough to convince me that stage three is really upon us. This may indeed be the first glimpses of stage three, but I am reserving judgement until I see more evidence. We will dive deeper into this trend example in just a moment.

Example - Social Gaming

Social Gaming is clearly in stage two. The graph could not be more text-book in nature. Social gaming, that fun diversion that companies like Zynga and others have capitalized on handsomely, is having (at the time of writing) a bit of a decline.

Social Gaming

Games online where you play with your friends, however, is not the fad that some would make it out to be. Notice how the decline in overall interest is not enough to return this trend to its pre-stage one levels. And as we know, sustainment is the difference between a fad and a trend. Social gaming will see stage three soon enough... just as soon as the first real utility is adopted by the mainstream public.

Example - Multi-Generational Workforce

Multi-generational workforces, that is, companies where there are actively several generations on the same working team, is a trend in stage two. This is an unusual trend because the reality is that multi-generational teams have been around a long time. They do not require technology to function, and whether or not there is social permission, it is going to happen. Time is the momentum here. What we see in the data for this trend is actually corporate awareness of it, and the associated desire to do something about it.

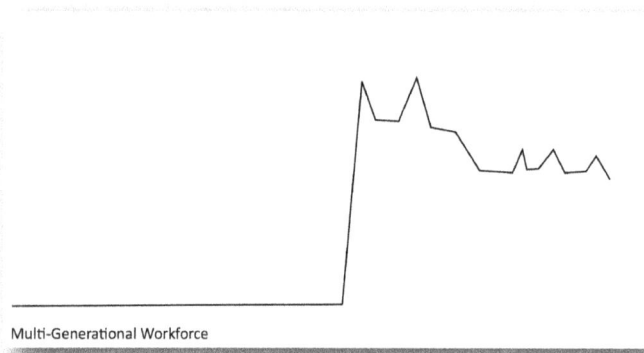

Multi-Generational Workforce

This trend is in stage two as managers have less interest in doing something about it... largely because they already figured out what to do. In line with that, Generational Reversal, which is a situation where younger managers lead older team members (a subset of multi-generational workforces), is a trend in stage three. We will focus on that in detail in later sections.

Example - Social Network Search

Social network search, that is, using your social network to search for that product you wanted to buy, or that movie you should go see this weekend, is a trend in stage two.

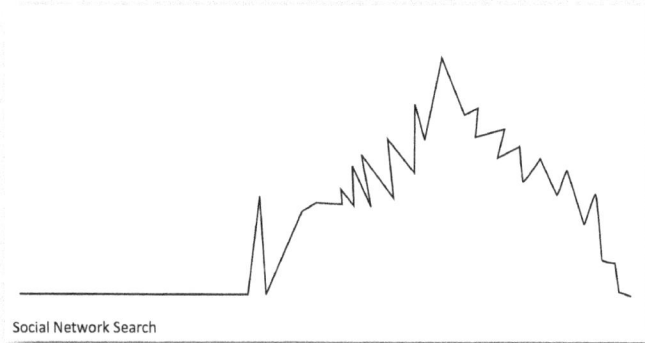

Social Network Search

The first prototypes of "social search" were rather exciting. They soon lost their luster, however, as people became annoyed with that level of closeness with their network, and the imperfections of technology. Just because I like to hang out at concerts with you, doesn't mean I trust your taste in movies or restaurants. This trend has a very disturbing data set as the overall interest has plummeted all the way back to pre-stage one levels. It was a good try, but this trend will have to fight hard to get to stage three. More likely, it will have to start over at stage one again. I am not ready to call it a fad, but time will tell.

Example: Under The Influence - Understanding The Stage Two Trend of Influence Marketing

Of the many ways to receive a marketing message, influence marketing has to be one of the most popular among customers yet one of the hardest forms of marketing to implement effectively because the message is transmitted through key individuals rather than directly to a target market. Word of mouth (WOM) marketing has always been the most effective form of advertising and, as noted on Wikipedia.org, "Word of mouth is a core part of the mechanics of influencer marketing. It identifies the individuals that have influence over potential buyers, and orients marketing activities around these influencers." Although the influence that results from a number of loose interactions among recipients of the message can be positive or negative, it involves less coercion from the marketer.

Currently, influence marketing is a trend in stage two. This is a precarious stage. Having seen prototype implementations, influence marketing is experiencing a drop in interest as we wait to see the first real utility and way of assessing how it works for businesses. In this example, we will explore the first stage of influence marketing, how it entered in stage two, and the perils of seeking stage three. Ultimately, it will probably get there, but it will take the emergence of an easy system that accurately assesses influence, and allows businesses to easily access influencers.

We have been under the influence of marketing messages since advertisements were first made. The "History of Influence" timeline on mashable.com shows how the power of peer influence began with the creation of the first recorded advertisement in 1704. Early progression was slow with ad agencies not being formed until more than a century later. Consumer reports were first published in 1936 so that potential customers could benefit from expert reviews of products and services. In 1940, a study by Lazerfeld and Katz, described on Wikipedia.org, concluded, "The majority of people are influenced by secondhand information and opinion leaders."

Radio and television advertising was very influential in the second half of the twentieth century along with the reliable word of housewives who connected through party plans like Tupperware. The integration of computer technology and search engines into a growing number of households in the 1990s added a new dimension to the way people could be influenced. And peer influence regained strength with the introduction of social networks like Facebook.

The transparency of social interactions and open publication of personal data also exposed potential customers to a new form of assault: data mining, but this also created an inroad for businesses to tailor their marketing practices and influence potential customers according to their personal preferences. As noted on the timeline, Twitter enables real-time sharing while Pinterest allows aggregation of products bolstering the effect of peer influence on purchasing decisions. According to an article by Josh Catone on mashable.com, "As the web's capacity for page views increases, marketers are becoming less interested in reaching as many people as possible, and more interested in reaching the right people." It was also noted in this article that context is very important and influence is not a numbers game.

The current form of influence marketing is relatively new and is increasingly being practiced commercially. By developing specific relationships between influencers and businesses, the message can be transmitted to key groups through word of mouth. Keller and Berry noted on Wikipedia.org, "Influencers are activists, are well-connected, have impact, have active minds, and are trendsetters." They added, "Exactly what is included in influencer marketing depends on the context (B2C or B2B) and the medium of influence transmission (online or offline, or both)." Having said that, the Forrester report statistic quoted on forbes.com shows where the power of persuasion lies: "In 80 percent of all B2C and B2B purchases there is some form of word-of-mouth recommendation at play during the purchase cycle." But as the author of the article noted, "A single tweet can make or break a company." Social bonds, real connections and reputation matter because people like to remain loyal to their friends.

Generally, statistics don't lie either. Shilpa Shree reported the results of a study by Technorati Media in an article on dazeinfo.com: "65 percent of top US brands reported participating in influencer marketing." Shree added, "64 percent of those deemed influencers by Technorati Media, had greater than average reach in a particular marketplace and made revenue from blogging, whether from ads on their site or sponsored endorsements from brands." Retail sites were found to be the most influential digital resource followed by brand sites when making a purchase. It was also found that blogs were considered more likely to influence an internet user's purchase decision than any other social channels, including Facebook. Around a third of respondents relied on blogs to guide them, but Facebook was a close contender for customers seeking guidance. But as Reuven Cohen noted on forbes.com, "A major concern is what happens once your friends and social contacts realize that they are being marketed to."

Technorati Media also found that brands were still spending about 75 percent of their digital marketing budget on display advertising, search and video, yet were only budgeting 10 percent for social. Of this 10 percent, half is spent on Facebook and the rest is divided among You Tube, Twitter, influence marketing and blog advertising. Facebook and Twitter were found to be the most popular platforms for bloggers; this is where most referrals and shares were generated. However, for consumers, You Tube, Facebook and Google + were found to be most popular.

The problem with influence marketing and probably the reason why it is only in trend stage two is that although online activity can be a core part of offline decision making, it is difficult to measure the direct correlation between the two and therefore justify advertising dollars. As noted by Mark W. Schaefer on cnbc.com, ""Influence" has been one of the most studied aspects of politics, marketing, sociology, and psychology and yet it has never really been measured in a statistically valid way." A number of companies offer online influence measurement but the doubters of the online-only approach described on Wikipedia.org, "Researching online sources misses critical influential individuals and inputs." In fact, "An overwhelming majority of WOM episodes (nearly 80%) ... occur in face-to-face interpersonal settings, while online WOM accounted for only seven to ten percent of the reported (WOM) episodes."

For small and medium-sized businesses, Forrester Research analyst, Michael Spayer, emphasized the need to identify and characterize influencers in the market and to establish criteria for ranking influencer impact on any decision making process. Accuracy of influencer scores is also a problem according to Sam Fiorella on spinsucks.com: "Inaccurate scores and faulty algorithms, lack of context represented in the scores, undefined relationships between influencers and followers, no real connection to sales results and improper use of scores by HR and customer service departments." He suggests public scoring may have prevented influence marketing from gaining acceptance.

Influence marketing is unlikely to go away. As Schaefer noted, "Influence has been democratized." And the use of this form of marketing has quickly moved down to a local level making it easier to identify influencers. Azeem Azhar, CEO of PeerIndex predicted in the forbes.com article, "Influence marketing is going to be huge – and will become an essential part of the marketing mix over the coming years. "

It is no longer realistic to passively market products and services to an anonymous customer base because the bottom line is that buyers trust other buyers, friends and experts that they know. From a business point of view, targeting influencers will counteract the growing tendency of prospective customers to ignore marketing.

To turn this trend into an advantage for your organization, consider the following. Influence marketing is a trend in stage two. That is, a pullback stage after first prototypes have peaked interest. Influence marketing is waiting for its first real utility. That is, a way for users to accurately identify influencers, and act on that resource in a way that makes business sense. Influence marketing has been in stage two for six years. As such, it will either die off now, or find its way to stage three. For stage three, influence marketing has to find real utility. Inaccurate influence scores, haphazard methodologies and undefined ROI are all holding it back. I would prepare and wait to use influence marketing. Have a plan ready to act and wait for the technology or methods that will be the real first utility, then act.

Conclusions

Stage two is the first real downturn for businesses associated with the trend. It can be very discouraging. At the end of this stage, however, once a real first utility is determined, and the technology is ready and polished, momentum will be restored and this trend will take off.

Stage 3 - First Utility

Overview

Stage 3, First Utility, is where we see the first real, polished and tested products, services, and monetization of a trend. It is a major growth stage and one of the two most important stage to be in, if you are looking for major growth and notoriety.

Momentum picks up significantly as hype, excitement and discussion about this new useful thing for immediate return on investment ripples through the business world. Businesses are interested for the potential direct return. Individuals are interested for careers and investments.

The utility in this stage is very well defined and focused. Customers know what to use it for, and they agree that it is the best possible use. First utilities are almost always associated with direct return on investment; an immediate boost to the bottom line. Frankly, that is what convinces users to try it again after the slump in stage two.

Example - Mobile Security

Mobile security is a trend in stage three. By looking at its graph, you might ask where the telltale stage two decline went. It is there, but it is very small. The mobile security industry did something right. They anticipated the first utility and pushed hard to get the technology and momentum there. As a result, stage two was minimal.

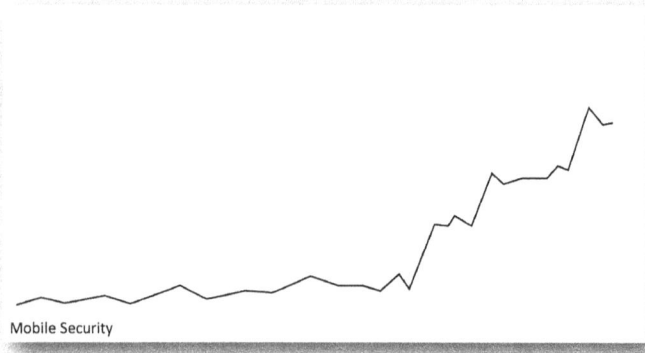

Mobile Security

They might, if they are smart (and I think they are), repeat that same process to minimize the inevitable stage four.

Example - Crowdsourcing

Crowdsourcing is a trend in stage three with an interesting graph. Stage one and two happened very fast, and stage three is dragging out. That is unusual as most trends progress through their stages in fairly equal intervals. With crowdsourcing, however, the practice of having the general public create your next big idea instead of an inside product team, the first utility has been so loved by businesses everywhere and consumers alike that they have not let it go. The usual complacency that would trigger stage four has not yet happened. That is not to say that is never will..... it just has not happened yet.

Crowdsourcing

Example: Young and In Charge - Managing The Stage Three Trend Of Generational Reversal

Increasingly, younger managers find themselves in charge of older team members. Generational reversal is a growing trend and one that is causing discomfort for everyone involved. Multi-generational teams are great for innovation, product development, marketing teams and much more. Older workers, however, may resent being led by younger counterparts. Actions like those reported by Amy MacMillan in an article in experience.com are common: "It's a mistake to come in and shake the place up without listening first." Lack of experience and demand for feedback lead to generalizations like the term "entitled" being branded around by baby boomers.

Many of the younger managers of today fall into the millennial category (also known as generation Y), which comprises individuals born between 1982 and the early 2000s. According to an article on management.fortune.cnn.com, "There's a significant disconnect in the workplace regarding how managers perceive the motivation and work ethic of millennials...but this is much more of a communication gap than a generation gap." However, as Lauren Friese and Cassandra Jarrett pointed out in their article in theglobeandmail.com, "These young managers, directors, vice-presidents, presidents and CEOs won't just be rearranging the furniture and hanging their diplomas in their new corner offices—they will be making sweeping changes to the way organizations and their people work." In this example, we explore the increasing trend of generational reversal and how to harvest advantage from the soil of objection.

According to survey results published in the management.fortune.cnn.com article, the biggest perceived difference between millennials and the baby boomer generation is technology. Another difference is the acceptability of the disappearing line between home and work. This more flexible approach to work hours is often interpreted by old-style managers to mean that newer managers want to do less work and have more time off. Also, the perceived higher expectations, noted by Friese and Jarrett, are that these "digital natives" expect to start as interns on Monday and be chief executive officers by Friday.

Baby boomers and earlier generations were raised in an era where a job was for life and they expected to spend years building skills and experience with the same employer in order to rise through the ranks. Incentives were offered for loyalty and pension plans were vested making them more attractive to those willing to devote their careers to one employer. Hard work was expected to lead to a management position in the long-term with the ultimate goal being a comfortable retirement at a respectable age. Results of the Generation Y survey conducted by Dr. Alison MacLeod found: "The idea that young managers want to work hard for a while and then take time off was not well supported; if anything, this desire was associated with more senior managers."

Until recently, most businesses operated with a hierarchical management structure. According to Friese and Jarrett, "Millennials aren't fond of the top-down leadership style that has until now dominated the professional world, preferring instead to collaborate in teams."

Today's young managers obviously have traits and characteristics that are highly valued by their employers; after all, that's why they were hired. But this does not necessarily mean they are "entitled". As noted in the management.fortune.cnn.com article, "They're probably the most misunderstood generation in the history of the world." They are not necessarily motivated by the desire to make money, but the need to make a difference. "What they're motivated by is making a contribution, feeling appreciated, and feeling like they're growing and learning."

With this trend currently in stage three, the first utility, this is an exciting time for both employers and job seekers. According to an article on go2hr.ca "The Internet has triggered the first industrial revolution in history to be led by the young." Millennials are transforming the workplace like never before. A greater percentage of women are now employed in managerial positions and mobile technology is changing the way people work. As noted in theglobeandmail.com article, "Recent surveys show that, like voice mail and snail mail before it, e-mail use is declining among younger millennials in favor of interacting on social networks and by text and instant messaging." Instant messaging is reported to increase productivity.

Also, clocking in at 9:00 a.m. and leaving at 5:00 p.m. is so 20th century. Flexible office hours and locations have led to a new type of work day where today's managers aren't concerned about how many hours employees work. "It won't matter in the new results-only work environment (ROWE), where employees are evaluated on performance, not presence." The added appeal of this to millennials is the potential for unlimited paid vacation time.

But the generational reversal seen by having these young managers in charge of older colleagues can create problems. Amy MacMillan wrote in her article on experience.com, "Age-related skepticism is a challenge for these new managers." The economictimes.com article noted," In a leadership role, there is a tendency to command respect, but when dealing with older professionals, it is important to first respect them for their experience." An experienced manager added on gradtogreat.com that despite having the potential to lead and to innovate, "These same characteristics that are valued so highly by your employer, may count for nothing with the people you are about to manage."

Home life will be an additional burden for many young managers. According to Friese and Jarrett, "Gen Y workers will have even more demanding family responsibilities than previous generations did, looking after not only their children but also their aging baby boomer parents." This "sandwich generation" is also likely to bury the concept of "a job for life" for good because they grew up during an era of mass job lay-offs in the 1980s and 1990s. As noted in the article in management.fortune.cnn.com, "They had seen the way their grandparents and uncles and aunts were treated by corporations and they didn't like it." This means that if a job lacks training opportunities and mentors sought out by millennials, they will move jobs every couple of years. However, MacLeod found, "31 per cent had been in their current jobs for more than 6 years and 32 per cent had been there between 3 and 5 years." She also noted that generation Y managers are only hired on short-term temporary contracts and face considerable financial pressures as a result of rising education costs and home prices.

MacLeod's study revealed some important factors in attracting young managers to new jobs: "Career development; working environment and values; lifestyle (i.e. pay, location and flexibility); and the need for change." She found, "Working environment, pay, and job security were also seen as very important, but these appeared to be secondary considerations." And critical for businesses looking to hire: "The overwhelming majority (97 per cent) is looking to build transferable skills."

Attitudes toward work and career will vary, but many young managers will seek out a good work-life balance; however, women and men may differ in their expectations. A flexible, progressive work environment is critical for promoting longevity in millennial managers. The writer of the go2hr.ca article noted that access to information and permission to express opinions was important to the generation Y workforce together with sensitivity to social issues by the hiring company. Young managers want immediate feedback and tailored development paths. If companies invest in these skills, these young managers might just stick around. As MacLeod found, "In some ways, young managers are a predictable herd, who may appear challenging, mercurial and demanding."

To turn generational reversal into an advantage for your organization, consider the following. Generational reversal is a trend in stage three. At the beginnings of this stage, this trend is poised for significant growth. Generational reversal is finding its first utility in innovation. Multi-generational teams are proving very useful indeed for new product and service ideas and more. Expect growth for the generational reversal trend for several years. Each stage of this trend seems to be taking about three years. Then, prepare to shorten stage four for generational reversal. Stage four will come about from increasing friction between generations. That friction, however, can be minimized by more swarm based organizational structures. Lastly, anticipate generational reversal's second utility, which I anticipate will be increased productivity as teams become more swarm oriented and older workers have an opportunity to mentor their younger leaders.

Example: The Smug And The Restless - Understanding Mobile Security As A Stage Three Trend

Mobile security, as a trend, is evolving very rapidly, more rapidly in fact than social media, including Facebook. According to a report on pandasecurity.com, "Lack of security awareness among cell phone users and carelessness are two of the most important risk factors for smartphones." The report added that a smartphone is far more than just a phone and should be treated more like a computer due to the valuable information it stores.

Mobile security started taking off in stage one during the summer of 2011 when, according to Richard Clooke, a leading security expert and editor of mobilesecurity.com, "Android had overtaken Symbian and J2ME to become the lead platform for mobile malware." Mobile security entered stage one hard core in early 2012, lasting about a year. Its second stage, the first period of decline, started in June of that year, and lasted a neat and tidy 11 months. This trend is interesting from the pure textbook nature of its behavior. We are not often so lucky to get such precise and obvious evolution. In this topic, we take a look at what is driving the mobile security trend, how long stage three will last (go ahead, guess!), and what you can expect in the years ahead for this fascinating trend.

In his history report Clooke said, "If we date the emergence of the smartphone back to 2000, with the launch of the Ericsson R380 and the Nokia 9210, it took over three years for the first examples of mobile malware to arrive." In 2004, researchers became aware of the first breach of mobile security: a worm called Cabir that infected Symbian devices. Cabir was fairly harmless but Clooke noted that in August 2004 a Trojan was found in illicit versions of the Symbian mobile game, Mosquito. Each time the game was played, the Trojan would send a premium SMS message to a certain number, making it the first mobile virus to take money from its victims. He added, "By mid-2005 Cabir was the foundation for whole families of Symbian viruses, including Pbstealer, a

Trojan that searched the phone's address book, then transmitted data obtained via Bluetooth to the first device in range." Skuller was another Symbian Trojan that deleted application files and replaced them with skull and crossbones alternatives.

These viruses were the first to spread across multiple platforms so by using your phone, you infected your PC. Clooke noted, "Malware always rises where there is a popular platform, a range of attack vectors and some means of monetization, and mobile devices offer all three." By 2006, cross-platform viruses were common, especially in weakly protected multi-media message services like Windows Mobile 2003. Symbian devices remained the most vulnerable until 2010 when Java led hackers to create the J2ME virus that infected the multiple platforms that supported Java.

Mobile malware exploded thereafter with many of the viruses causing SMS fraud. Although Google's Android operating system was introduced in 2008, consumer uptake was slow for the first couple of years. By 2010 Android's hackers began to take advantage of its weak security and the first Android Trojans invaded. As Clooke wrote, "Google's open model made it possible for a range of app stores, some illicit, to operate and made it easy for malware to use social engineering methods to propagate." By the end of 2011, Clooke said that iPhones had mostly been spared, apart from Jail-broken iPhones. But, hackers were stepping up their game by obtaining mobile authorization codes to gather data from users' PCs to access their bank accounts.

The National Cyber-Security Advisory Council studied technical, financial and historical aspects of the mobile market to find what smartphone models were most likely to become the next big target for cyber-crooks. The CNCCS - Smartphone Malware Report found that the creation of flat-rate data plans from operators played a major role in popularizing this type of device and subsequently also increased use of its associated services – from email to online banking. The report noted, "Android-based devices are on the rise and gaining market share on its rivals. iOS is on the decline despite maintaining market leadership. BlackBerry has dropped slightly in popularity over the last few years." Currently, Clooke noted, "Android's huge market-share – 70 percent of smartphone sales in fourth-quarter 2012, according to Gartner— guarantees that it will be the leading malware platform for the foreseeable future," Obviously, the most popular devices are the ones most likely to be hacked.

The CNCCS report found communication channels to be the biggest concern with Smartphones, "They are more vulnerable than traditional PCs and can be subjected to various attack vectors – SMS, Bluetooth, WiFi, Web browsers, applications and email—an aspect that can result in the proliferation of malicious code targeting these platforms." Just because you carry phones with you doesn't mean they are invincible. Although, the report noted, "There are more than 60 million known malicious programs for PCs as opposed to 600 for smartphones," this is not a time to be complacent. Blackberry, Nokia and Apple take responsibility for the applications available on their App Stores, whereas Android delegates security to developers. However, even when developers are responsible, functionality of code can be impaired when used by third party applications. Trusting app stores for security is therefore not enough.

Security is surprisingly a tough sell to users of mobile technology and Smartphones. Even though more than ten years has passed since the first attacks on cellphones, Roger A. Grimes said on infoworld.com, "Most cellphone vendors still don't stop these types of attacks." Grimes believes that cellphone code has more exploit vectors per line than today's normal computer code and fewer built-in default protections making it very easy to create malware for mobile platforms. Luis Corrons, technical director of PandaLabs said, "One of the major challenges security vendors face is user mobility." And because, as noted on lookout.com, thousands of never-before-imagined mobile services sprouted up overnight, hackers view mobile phones as a one-stop shop for identity theft and fraud.

With this in mind, users can develop good practices to protect themselves from malware: use a PIN or password to restrict access; configure the smartphone to automatically lock after being idle for a minute; check the reputation of apps before installing them and read security permission requests carefully; disable Bluetooth, infrared or Wi-Fi when not in use; back-up your data and encrypt sensitive information, or store it elsewhere; check your account activity frequently and get your phone blocked if it is lost or stolen; be wary of files or links received from unsolicited email or SMS and delete them if in doubt and avoid using untrusted Wi-Fi networks.

Future trends were outlined by Ken Huang and James Hewitt in an HDI report:

- Near Field Communications (NFC) will gain more momentum for payment, ticketing, and check-in devices

- Payments through smartphones will replace plastic cards and keys

- 4G will replace 3G because it is faster, is a higher quality and has added security features

- WiMax (Worldwide Interoperability for Microwave Access) and WiFi will co-exist for the foreseeable future and more WiFi hotspots will attract more security breaches

- Federal Government will continue to adopt apps and mobile apps will become more mature

- iPhones, iPads, and iPods will have NFC and more secure channels will exist for NFC

- A large number of mobile applications will be built for multiple platforms, but apps will be more vulnerable to hacking

- The market for mobile devices will consolidate with time and data protection will improve

- 2014 will witness over 3 billion mobile users worldwide

Meanwhile the impact of mobile malware will deepen with more emphasis on financial gain. Attacks will be directed toward the second authentication factor (cell phones) used by online banking services. According to Grimes, "The objective is now to multiply the effects of their infections and attacks, affecting as many devices as possible." Unless, of course, finger print swipes and facial recognition prove to be a reliable defense.

To turn this trend into an advantage for your business, consider the following. Mobile security is a textbook example of trend stages. Neat and tidy stages at predictable intervals; it does not come any better than this. Mobile security is a trend in stage three. This is a growth stage fueled by its first utility. Mobile security's third stage should last about one year. Expect mobile security to hit stage four, a downturn right after that. Stage four is a pullback stage based on limitations and high customer expectations. To shorten this stage, anticipate the second utility for Mobile Security. I believe it will be on the hardware side of the industry.

Conclusions

Stage three is a time of significant growth and excitement. Companies are made, investors flourish, and careers spark We are a fickle bunch, however, and soon enough we are complacent and spoiled. The first utility is just not enough anymore, and social permission drops off as the public complains about how limited this trend really is. This will trigger stage four.

Stage 4 - Limitations

Overview

Stage 4, Limitations, is where businesses acting on this trend must get clever. Interest, and possibly revenues at this stage have pulled back yet again. It is another frightening stage for business owners and investors alike; but not quite as scary as stage two was. Smarter now, we realize that customers are just looking for more focus and a bit more utility.

Momentum stalls in this stage as headlines suggest that maybe this trend is past its peak and not the great thing we all thought it might be. It is really just a matter of complacency. Having grown accustomed to the first utility, we are bored. It is not enough anymore.

The first utility was very good and offered great return. Now we want more. Now we wish that this trend could fix what else is wrong in our businesses and lives.

The technology is so well in place by this stage that we almost expect great things and are disappointed when we are not constantly amazed.

Yes, stage four is a brat. It is like a toddler who just had a cookie and now demands a whole plate full more.

Example - Crowdfunding

Crowdfunding is a trend in stage four, that does not look like a trend in stage four. This is another case of reserving judgement until I have more evidence. The brief pullback seen as this trend's stage four, I believe, is not quite over. The reason I am not convinced, is that the second utility has not appeared.

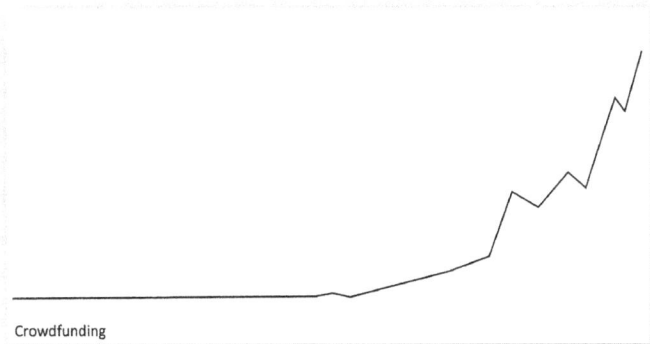

Crowdfunding

Momentum is high for this trend and always has been, which helps to shorten stages two and four, but the lack of a second utility suggests the growth will not be totally sustainable. Time will tell. As of the time of this writing, I am leaving this trend in stage four. We will discuss it in more detail in a moment.

Example - Augmented Reality

Augmented reality is a trend in stage four that is a bit more obvious. This trend found a great first utility in the gaming world. Now, bored with that, customers crave something more.

Augmented Reality

They are likely to get that great second utility; but not until the technology is more finished, and fashionably acceptable.

Example - Voice Recognition

Voice recognition is a trend in stage four, that might look like something far worse. The data for voice recognition systems is only available starting in 2005. The trend, however, started much earlier than that. What we see here in the graph is the very top of stage three, and the decline of stage four.

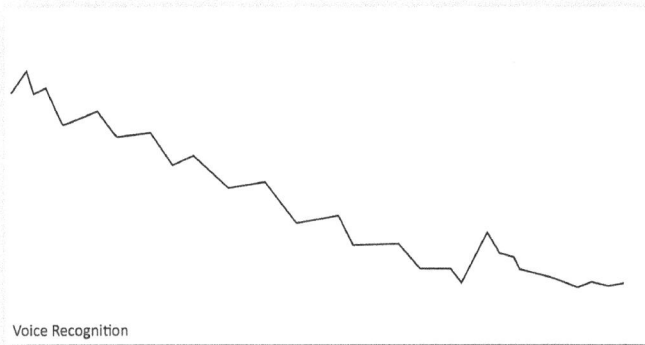

Voice Recognition

An attempt at stage five growth fools us a bit in this data but the growth is not sustained; keeping this trend squarely in stage four for a while longer. We will talk in depth about this trend in a moment.

Example - Virtual Teams

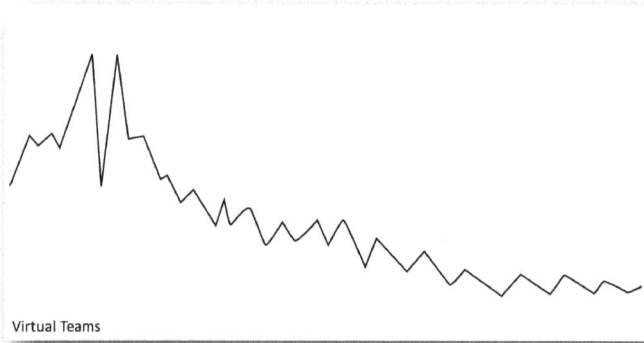

Virtual Teams

Virtual teams (as in teams working inside your company) is a trend in stage four as well. A double spike in stage three shows how business interest and worker interest fought to keep the trend alive. The decline, however, of stage four cannot be denied.

Employer frustration with accountability pushed this trend into stage four. These limitations, and a lack of technology to fix them, has kept the trend in stage four for longer than might be expected. Technology for freelancer and virtual team accountability, however, is nearly complete and I expect this trend to take off again into the growth of stage five that so many businesses will benefit from.

Example: Crowdfunding - Tracking This Stage Four Trend

Crowdfunding is an evolving trend. Some say it is old news and some say it is the future of fundraising for companies. I think it is both. This trend is undergoing stages just like any other and is a trend in stage four, that is, the limitations stage. It is pulling back under increased competition combined with major limitations to the current form of use but not yet having seen its second real utility. In this example we will talk about the right things to do now, to create an advantage from this particular stage four trend.

According to wikipedia.org, crowdfunding, also known as crowd financing, equity crowdfunding or hyper funding, describes the collective effort of individuals who pool their money to support people or organizations in need of funding. The popularity of the process has been boosted by a weak economy that has made loans difficult to secure and a rise in the use of social media networks that has made spreading the word easier. Many good ideas would otherwise go to waste without the funding required for people to develop the idea. To the naysayers, crowdfunding may seem like a gamble, but it also demonstrates evidence of public support for an idea or organization and assists growth of the idea through on- and offline networks.

Early types of crowdfunding were used in the 19th and 20th century to finance home purchases in the form of group housing, community housing and cooperatives. Although the term, "crowdfunding", may not have been used, charity events and political rallies have always solicited donations using the same process. More recently, around the start of the new millennium, the music industry adopted crowdfunding as a way to sell music and pay for tours through an American-based company, ArtistShare. Since then, crowdfunding has evolved to encompass many different ventures around the globe; film-makers, journalists, bloggers and non-profits were among the early experimenters of this funding process. Today, according to wikipedia.org, "There are over 500 crowdfunding platforms all over the world and it has come to the point where project creators need to do their own due diligence in order to understand which platform is the best one to use depending on the type of project that they want to launch."

Until recently, different rules applied to businesses seeking funding from the "crowd". In the 1930s, laws were passed to prohibit businesses from soliciting funds from individuals or investors that were not accredited money lenders. The Securities and Exchange Commission (SEC) was thus formed to protect investors and promote efficient use of capital funds. But this led to complications in the modern world. As Sherwood Neiss, an entrepreneurship enthusiast, explained in an article on miamiherald.com, "Seeking investment capital from the public is illegal unless you go through a costly registration process with the Securities & Exchange Commission." He added, "The old rules needed to change. However, it required updating the security laws to the Internet Age."

Last year, as noted in wikipedia.org, "President Barack Obama signed the JOBS (Jumpstart Our Business Startups) Act, legislation that effectively lifted a previous ban against public solicitation for private companies raising funds." However, businesses that wish to sell equity stakes online to investors must still use only registered websites because, without regulation, crowdfunding could quickly return to unsavory operators selling bogus stocks to amateur investors. Equity-based crowdfunding also evolved for business start-ups so that investors would receive ownership, or a small part, of the businesses in which they invest. If the business succeeds, the shares increase in value; but if the business tanks, then the investor loses out too. Another bonus, according to Jeremy Quittner on inc.com, "New analytics tools have made crowdfunding sites an excellent source for feedback on your business." Entrepreneurs can track their search-engine rankings and the impact their social-media presence has on attracting crowdfunding. Kevin Lawton noted on venturebeat.com, "The transparency and social networking dynamics of crowdfunding have been excellent at keeping fraud near zero, to the point where heavy regulation will work against this new economic machine."

Crowdfunding has also gained traction in the science field. According to a blog post by Anthony Salvagno on scienceexchange.com, platforms like SciFundChallenge and petridish.org have provided support and public recognition for science research. He reported that this was encouraging, "While crowdfunding may not be the complete solution it does present an alternative means for research support, with improved transparency and public engagement, than existing mediums of support."

In 2012, Ryan Caldbeck reported on techradar.com, "By the end of this year, there will be an estimated 500+ crowdfunding platforms worldwide, which is up 60 percent from 2011, driven by the explosion of equity-based portals after the passage of the JOBS Act." Even though there are now numerous crowdfunding sites, some have gained more popularity than others like Kickstarter and Microventures. And, according to a post on dailydot.com, the top three most influential crowdfunding campaigns completed with Kickstarter in 2012 were Pebble Technology, whose smartwatch raised $10,266,845; Double Fine Adventure gaming, which raised $3,336,371 and Amanda Palmer & the Grand Theft Orchestra's new album, which raised $1,192,793—quite impressive considering none of these organizations anticipated such success.

So, if it's that easy, shouldn't everyone be doing it? Well, maybe. In order to generate interest and solicit funds, businesses have to release details of the project and, as noted on wikipedia.org, "This exposes the promoter of the idea to the risk of the idea being copied and developed ahead of them by better-financed competitors." Also, some operations may find it difficult to make a success of the business once the funds have been raised. "Managing communications with a large number of possibly disappointed investors and supporters can be a substantial, and potentially diverting, task." This could be the stumbling block that explained the results of a survey reported in an article on wsj.com, "In a November survey of 740 small-business owners, with between $1 million and $20 million in annual revenue, only 21 percent said they were aware of the JOBS Act. Just three percent of small businesses said they felt they would benefit from equity crowdfunding, according to the survey, by The Wall Street Journal and Vistage International Inc."

So, after the initial burst of enthusiasm, it seems that crowdfunding is definitely in trend stage four. After the initial excitement, the process is being subject to a reality check and is now gaining traction before progressing into trend stage five, the final major stage of growth. Research statistics reported by Caldbeck showed, "Massolution estimates the crowdfunding industry (equity + donation + lending +reward crowdfunding) will grow from $1.5 billion in 2011 to $2.8 billion in 2012." Caldbeck also predicted that angel groups will embrace equity crowdfunding and donation based crowdfunding sites will differentiate or die.

But Caldbeck remained cautious because he believes the JOBS Act is likely to require that equity based portals register with FINRA as broker dealers, therefore he said, "2013 will be the year of consolidation, not the explosive growth so many others predict."

The future of crowdfunding is still a little uncertain because the SEC rules have not yet been finalized. In December 2012, Ina Paiva Cordle reported in the article on miamiherald.com that Neiss said, "We don't expect the rules to be issued by year-end, but are hoping it will happen in the first quarter of 2013. Then the SEC will consider public comments and come out with the final rules, hopefully by the end of the second quarter of 2013." So, we will continue to monitor this trend.

To create advantage from crowdfunding, consider the following. Crowdfunding is a stage four trend. That is, having enjoyed one real utility, it has pulled back under the weight of limitations awaiting its second real reason to exist. Crowdfunding could see a big boost in early 2013 at it moves into stage five - second utility. Anticipate the next use for crowdfunding. Big brands will benefit most from crowdfunding, by using it to fund new product development from an already existing fan base. Startups will have continued difficulty with crowdfunding, however and may have to wait until stage seven to find it useful.

Example: Talking Back - Understanding The Stage Four Trend Of Voice Based Systems

"Welcome to ABC Products; for English, press one. Please listen carefully and use your key pad to select from the following options: to place an order, press one; to enquire about an existing order, press two; to update your account information, press three; to fly to the moon and back, press four..." Oh, wait; maybe that should be..."To preserve your sanity by speaking with a customer service agent, press zero." Ah, finally, a person! But hang on, "Your call will be answered in the order in which it was received and you are caller number seven. Please hold the line; your call is important to us"...Sound familiar? If it doesn't, then you must have evolved on a different planet.

However, voice based systems have come a long way since the days of automated answering services. Today's systems can recognize you, check the tone of your voice, pull up your records and funnel angry customers quickly to well trained customer service reps. These state of the art systems are not widely used, but soon may be. In this topic, we explore the stage four trend of voice based systems, where they are going and what you need to know.

Interactive Voice Response (IVR) systems are in stage four, that is, the decline after first utility. Having found their first utility with basic customer service applications, customers grew weary of their annoyance. A general revolt among the populace cried out to talk to a real human. Now nearing the end of stage four, these systems are seeking their second major utility to drive them into the growth expected in stage five.

Advances in telephone technology gave rise to automated response systems. Without the Touch-Tone keypad introduced by AT&T in 1963, we may never have had to engage in dialogue with a machine, but who could have imagined that the act of talking to another human being would disappear along with the rotary dial? According to Wikipedia.org, call centers began using IVR technology to automate tasks in the 1970s but high usage costs prohibited most businesses from embracing the new technology.

As more competitors entered the market in the 1980s and digitized voice data was introduced, the costs came down. By the late 1990s, call centers were investing in Computer Telephony Integration with IVR systems and calls handled by automated responses became more main-stream. This meant that callers were now able to interact with an IVR through both speech and telephone keypads. As Ken Landoline, principal with Synergy Research Group said in an article on crmbuyer.com, "The last quantum leap for IVRs was the shift from touchtone to speech interface."

According to a white paper compiled by aspectsoftware.com, the most basic technology uses voice prompts and touch tone key pads. More advanced technology features text-to-speech, speech recognition and speech verification. Text-to-speech (TTS) applications have been around since the early 1990s and the paper noted, "TTS is now more advanced so TTS words and phrases can blend seamlessly with recorded prompts and you can make individually tailored suggestions in a friendly, human voice."

At the next level, speech recognition applications "understand" the words and phrases of the callers so more complex requests can be dealt with. This is a popular option for businesses with high call volumes because speech recognition can reduce the time required to prompt the caller for information by up to 1000 per cent resulting in huge savings in staffing costs.

The paper by Aspect Software describes speaker verification as the most advanced application which simplifies the identification of the caller without asking for a PIN or ID number. Speaker verification uses the caller's unique voice print to recognize him or her and is very customer-friendly.

Taking into consideration Aspect Software's considerable bias, the benefits of IVRs are clear: they can reduce wait times, handle routine inquiries and free up agents for more complex requests. IVRs extend service hours to 24/7, 365 days per year and offer privacy for sensitive inquiries. Increasing service hours increases revenue and extends market reach across any time zone. Overall, IVRs reduce overheads of staffing and facility costs.

But, you need to consider customer satisfaction. Research conducted by Assistant Professor Liel Leibovitz at NYU reported on blogs.aberdeen.com, found, "Customers have negative perceptions toward IVR, considering it the least preferred medium when trying to reach customer service." And Aberdeen's data showed, "Only 51% of incoming calls are resolved by the first agent and that nearly 20% of all incoming calls go unanswered, significantly impacting customer satisfaction." With only half of calls answered by IVR being resolved, cost-savings are not so significant.

Arie Goldshlager noted in an article on quora.com that the intelligence and contextual use of data to make speech recognition personalized and effective has to improve for voice technology to be more acceptable. Goldshlager wrote, "Creating personas of customers has the potential to drastically improve the effectiveness of voice technologies in use today." With this in place, routine customer service tasks would be more streamlined. She added, "The level of customer satisfaction achieved with them will be increasingly determined by how well these systems add contextual and persona-based intelligence to each interaction."

Jay E. Coop expressed dissatisfaction on ezinearticles.com, "In looking at today's speech IVRs, it's painfully clear that very little real progress has actually occurred." However, many of the issues with voice technology seem to crop up with callers who don't like IVRs in the first place. As Landoline said, "They are already going into the transaction with the idea that they will be inconvenienced or won't get what they want." And even with such mature technology, there will always be glitches. The writers of the Aspect paper believe that customer dissatisfaction mostly results from automating the wrong applications and claims that most companies use IVRs to reduce staffing costs despite knowing IVRs reduce customer satisfaction.

These and other hiccups like accents and background noise are what have kept this trend in stage four for so long. Leah Eyler, a business analyst, said on crmbuyer.com, "The first order of business, I think, for many companies, is to focus on getting their existing technology to work correctly—and then focus on new developments in this space." There are better tools for detecting problems and "customer experience analytics," or CEA can be used to analyze customer experiences.

Aspect makes various recommendations for successful implementation of IVR systems but the most useful advice is to avoid creating endless loops in the system by referring callers to an agent as soon as responses are not recognized and explaining clearly how to get help and go back to previous menus.

According to an article by Kate Legget on forrester.com, voice is still the primary communication channel used, but is closely followed by self-service channels, especially with growing usage of mobile technology. Legget also indicated a trend toward more agile services because channel preference is changing rapidly: "Breaking down communication silos within and outside of customer service and standardizing the resolution process and customer service experience across communication channels and touch points." She predicted, "The range of channels for proactive outbound will increase, and will include service alerts, workarounds, customized cross-sell and up-sell offers." Whereas, Coop alluded to a new tier of technology: IVRs powered by artificial intelligence. And the biggest trend anticipated by Legget in the Forrester report: "Collaboration is becoming a corporate mindset." She said to expect customer service organizations to start moving forward with more holistic measurement programs for communication channels and touch points.

To turn this stage four trend into an advantage for your business, consider the following. Voice based systems are a stage four trend. That is, they have pulled back from customer frustration after some moderate first utility. Voice based systems need to find a second utility.Voice based systems may languish in stage four for years as they wait for the technology to catch up. Understanding customer emotion will put voice systems in stage five. Most importantly, I am avoiding voice based systems until stage five.

Conclusions

At this stage, finding the second real utility is key. You cannot prevent this stage from happening, but you can make it shorter and less painful. If you can find the second real utility, you can drive the trend into stage five and re-start the engines of growth.

Stage 5 - Second Utility

Overview

Stage 5, Second Utility, is where we see the largest amount of solid business growth for any given trend. Businesses established in stage three will grow to major market competitors in stage five; especially if they were clever enough to anticipate and prepare to offer the second utility that drives this stage.

Momentum picks back up as headlines and individuals return to their original excitement. Those who previously panned the trend as over in stage four now are best friends with the CEOs that are taking stage five companies to new levels of growth.

Technology is well in hand to make it happen, and businesses acting on this trend seem to really be solidifying their place in the world. Everything goes smoothly. This is the golden moment for businesses who make this trend the basis of their offerings. Venture capitalists tend to get involved here if they prefer less risky offerings, but still want significant growth.

In stage five, a second utility emerges that indirectly offers return on investment for businesses and individuals. It might be a marketing channel, human resources boost, or other operationally inclined use.

Not all trends, however, are a good thing. Our favorite trend in stage five is cyber warfare. Let's take an in depth look at how cyber warfare came to be in stage five, and why that is ultimately great news.

Example: Cyber Warfare - Anticipating Setbacks For This Stage Five Trend

Cyber Warfare

Cyber warfare affects your company's operations in every area from intellectual property, to customer data, sales, and more. As Rob Shein, cyber security architect for HP's Security and Privacy Professional Services division, said on infosectoday.com, "While non-kinetic warfare offers the potential for impact without loss of life, it also broadens the battlefield in a fashion that has not been seen since the advent of the airplane."

The bottom line for businesses is that it can cost your organization millions and potentially billions. In cyber warfare, attacks on civilian businesses are considered equally as aggressive as attacks on military targets. As Shein noted, "There exist two primary objectives that compete for primacy in the context of information warfare. One is the control of information, either in the sense of gaining access to it or denying access to it. The other is influence over that information."

The bad news is that cyber attack is a trend, not a fad. The good news is that it is in stage five, the second utility. The first utility of cyber warfare resulted in servers being taken down; the second utility centered on theft of information and money. But there is a lot of worldwide competition in the attack industry and companies have had enough.

Once businesses mount a strong enough defense, which will thwart the majority of methods, the trend will enter stage six and attackers will have to retool to determine the long term effects of cyber attacks. Hopefully, this will be a long, painful decline. In this topic, we cover the current stage of cyber warfare, what it means for your business, what will take this trend out of commission for a while, and what you need to do to be ready.

Worm attacks were prevalent back in the seventies and have become increasingly sophisticated in recent years. According to the History of Cyber Warfare Timeline published on online.lewisu.edu, just a decade ago, worm viruses compromised computers which subsequently became members of the Botnet farms. Then in 2005, the intensity of cyber warfare deepened when the computer network of the world's largest oil company, Saudi ARAMCO, was destroyed and the hard drives of 30,000 of its PCs were wiped out. As detailed in an article on vanityfair.com, the hackers who identified themselves as Islamic left a calling card: "The hackers lit up the screen of each machine they wiped with a single image, of an American flag on fire." The attack was reportedly directed at the Saudi government for its support of crimes and atrocities, but White House officials determined the attack was payback by Iran for Western government's ongoing cyber warfare against Iran's nuclear program; Saudi was merely a proxy.

The unseen warfare has since escalated and the target range has increased to include major entities like The Pentagon, NASA, Ebay, Microsoft, Google and Apple. According to Shein, the Fourth Geneva Convention may have protected innocent civilians from kinetic warfare but non-kinetic cyber warfare seems to circumvent this kind of protection.

Additionally, this kind of warfare is attractive because it is cheap and it is difficult for victims to attribute blame, therefore a conventional military response on a larger scale is unlikely. Many attacks are unsophisticated and are carried out by civilian hackers that are sympathetic to a nation-state.

Private organizations have limited defenses beyond normal security practices and all may be targets. Shein described the three forms of threat: "One, an organization that is smaller, relatively immature in information security measures, and thus useful as a stepping stone in attacks on other organizations. The second is of organizations that, for some reason, have gained the attentions of groups with nationalist, environmental, or other motivators. The third contains organizations which themselves are tightly linked to national drivers and infrastructure."

Currently, according to an article on engadget.com, Wall Street banks conduct cyber warfare drills to devise strategic plans for a variety of scenarios. After a year of hard-core debate the Pentagon has also drawn up action plans to defend against cyber attacks. And, as noted in tradearabia.com, governments are purchasing additional monitoring tools to enable access to targeted mobile devices in an attempt to stay ahead of cyber criminals. However, this is proving to be controversial.

As noted by Shein, managing the risks is tough, "Even the largest multinational private companies have never had more than a limited capability to address the challenges of warfare, even when operating in conflict regions." He added, "The current Obama administration in the United States is making bold moves toward a national policy to improve the cyber security in the private sector." The population may not be suffering loss of life from cyber warfare, but manipulative tactics by hackers may trigger larger conflicts or adversely affect ongoing diplomatic negotiations between nations. New enabling technologies may also pose a great risk to things like the national power grid.

When smaller, less well-defended targets are used for staging against more prominent ones, the source of attack may be obscured therefore allowing further damage to prevail before discovery. Problems can arise when large, multi-national corporations are tied to foreign nations through the outsourcing of their manufacturing processes. Shein wrote, "This almost provides a kind of hostage situation whereby an attack upon them would inevitably (and quickly) incur harm upon the attacking nation." This would result in harm to the economies on both sides of the attack. Shein noted, "The phrase, "Globalization stops wars," is at least as true with cyber warfare as it is with kinetic warfare."

However, "China is by far the most active transgressor," wrote the author of an article in economist.com, "The other biggest offenders are Russia and, recently, Iran." But America is not just an innocent victim; the article added, "Either America, Israel or the two working together almost certainly hatched the Stuxnet worm." Experts maintain that in cyber warfare the attacker has the advantage. General Keith Alexander, head of Cyber

Command and the National Security Agency, was quoted saying, "Although America has better offensive cyber-capabilities than almost anybody, its defenses get only three out of ten." As noted in the economist.com article, "Often the weakest link is their professional advisers, such as law firms or bankers who have access to sensitive data." Regardless of the handling of information, attribution remains difficult and relies on context, motive and an assessment of capabilities as much as technology.

But America is pulling out all the stops. Warren Stroebel and Deborah Charles wrote on Reuters.com, "The future of U.S. warfare is rising in the shape of the new $358 million headquarters for the military's Cyber Command." The main focus is defense but plans will be in place to switch to attack mode if the nation is subject to cyber assault. Much of this information is classified; however, even though defense budgets have been cut, "Cyber spending would grow by $800 million, to $4.7 billion." And it takes time to train cyber warriors. Alexander said, "Cyber Command's new teams won't be fully ready until at least 2016 due to military bureaucracy and because it takes time to pull together people with the special skills needed." Raphael Mudge, a private cyber security expert said in the economist article, "Cyber security really is a cat and mouse game." He added, "That kind of thinking can't be taught. It has to be nurtured."

Meanwhile, Kaspersky Lab noted that 2012 was the year of explosive growth of mobile malware, therefore it predicted that 2013 would be the year for increased attacks on mobile devices especially because so much personal and corporate data is stored on Smartphones and tablets that tend not to be as well protected as traditional computers.

To turn this trend into an advantage for your organization, consider the following. Cyber warfare is a trend, not a fad. It is not going away anytime soon. Cyber warfare is a trend in stage five. It may seem overwhelming right now, but soon enough will enter stage six, a stage of significant difficulty for those who would attack. Cyber warfare is on the verge of decline. This decline will be forced by a large number of highly effective technologies for defending your infrastructure that are coming out now and over the next year. Position your business for secure operation. Don't be lazy about it. Even in stage six, complacency about cyber security is naive. Don't rest easy. The decline will not last long and soon enough we will, as organizations, have to evolve again.

Conclusions

Stage five is where many business executives want to be. Life is good here, revenues are high, and products are well established. Enter the competition... and plenty of it; to ring in the dreaded stage six.

Stage 6 - The Competitive Tidal Wave

Overview

Stage 6, The Competitive Tidal Wave, is where we see giants fall (or so it would seem). The rush of competition threatens to commoditize the offering. Sometimes it does indeed commoditize it. Sometimes it is just an illusion. At this stage, everything seems to be against the trend and the businesses associated with it.

Customers, once again, become complacent and spoiled and complain about the little things that could be improved. Often in this stage, the word on the street will sound like, "It would be perfect, if they would only..." The competition is acting on those "if onlys." Momentum in this stage is not just stalled, it is downright negative. Headlines blast the businesses involved as over, done and finished.

Utility is still there. First and second utility are still in effect and still selling, but something has gone wrong. At this point, customers are not screaming for a new utility, they are screaming for stability - they want to know what this trend and this business will be for them years and sometimes decades from now.

Example - Visualization Software

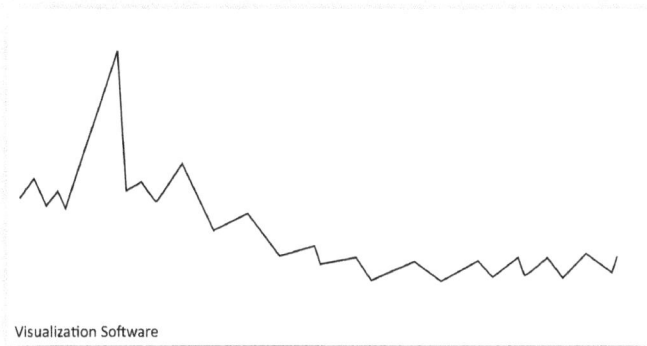

Visualization Software

Visualization software, that is, tools to visualize big data, is a trend in stage six. The trend has been developing for quite a long time, so what we see here in the graph is the last of stage five's growth, and the whole of stage six. This trend is currently stalled out and having a lot of difficulty, from a technology perspective and a human user perspective. We will go in depth on this trend in just a moment.

Example - Tablets

This may surprise a lot of people, but tablet computers are a trend in stage six. Yes, that includes iPads and Android devices alike. Trend graphs do not come much cleaner and perfect than this. Look now, as it may be the only time you ever see such an obvious graph.

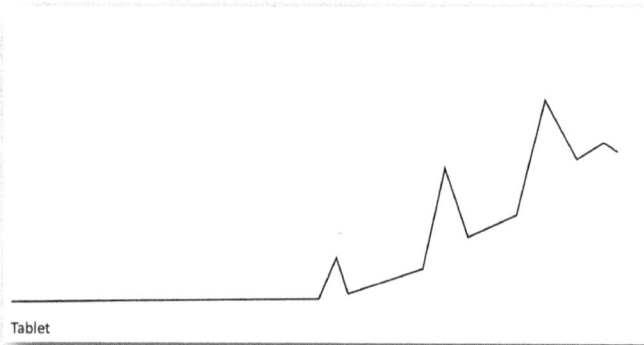

Tablet

Granted, sales are still hot, revenues are doing well, and it is hard to see this trend as having the largest setback of its existence. For some trends, however, setbacks are small and not nearly as painful as we might expect. This is the case with tablets. They are in fact retooling for longevity... Even the iPad isn't quite there yet.

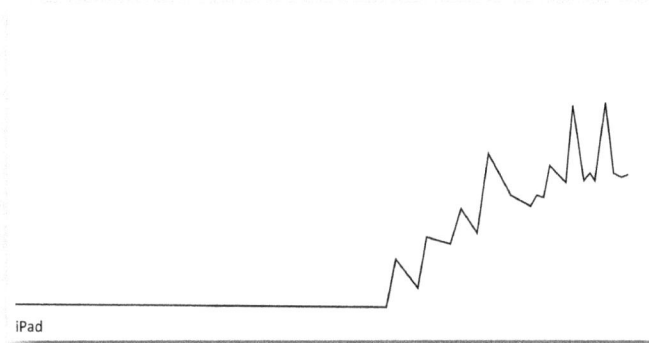

iPad

This trend nearly qualifies as a supertrend (one that flattens out its pullback stages). But not quite. Soon enough, tablets will find their more final form, and enter stage seven, that coveted stage of long term steady growth.

Example - Terrorism

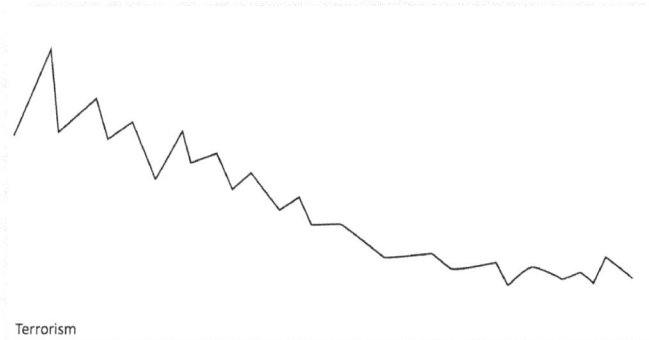

Terrorism

Not all trends are technical. Terrorism is a great example of a trend in stage six. The practice of terrorism has been around a very long time, with a recent surge of what might seem like growth in the western world. Terrorism, however, is facing a major retooling. What will it look like long-term?

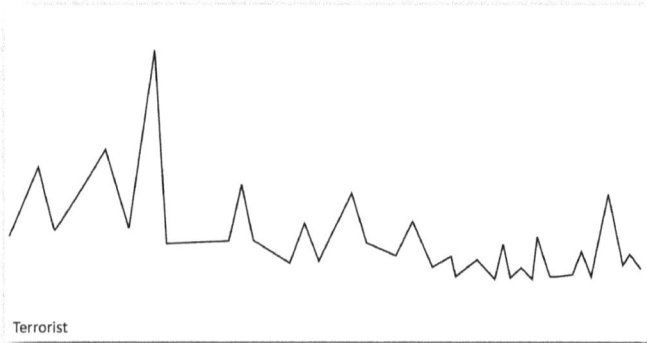

Terrorist

More interestingly, is the issue of being a terrorist. When we look at the graph for terrorist, we do not see a trend at all... we see a fad. Notice the spiky nature of the interest levels that never really gain altitude. Fads require media coverage and buzz to keep going. Kill the buzz, kill the fad. That says some interesting things about the future of terrorist activity that I will leave to governments and military interests to interpret.

Example - Business Incubators

Business incubators, in the traditional sense, are a trend in stage six as well.

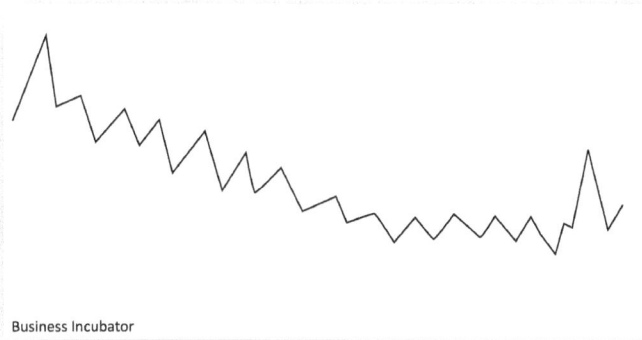

Business Incubator

There is a spike of potential that suggests stage seven might very soon be confirmed. We will go in depth on this trend in just a moment.

Example - Facebook

Facebook is always a fun example. They issued their IPO about 6 months after entering stage six. For the record, that is 6 months too late. We are all aware of the consequences that ensued. Facebook, until stage six, was a supertrend, having flattened out stages two and four for a stellar rise all the way to the peak of stage five. The lesson here is that stage six cannot be avoided completely, even for supertrends. Facebook will find their way, retool for longevity, and ultimately come out on top. It will just have to endure a little pain until then.

Facebook

Example: Data Visualization - Tracking This Stage Six Trend

The large majority of all trends go through seven distinct stages. Data visualization is a trend in stage six. Over many years, we saw data visualization capture interest with its first prototypes, feel the sting of limitations, find several utilities and come back into vogue and now it seems it's time to retool for longevity. The world, at the moment, is trying to figure out what this trend will look like for the long haul. The space is packed in with competitors and as many different ways to visualize data as there are people who want to visualize it. And that is the thing—data visualization is a personal activity. What gives one person an "ah ha" moment does not necessarily light the fire of another. Because of this, there is not going to be a one size fits all solution. That will keep this trend in stage six for a longer time than most trends. There may, however, be a common process and larger set of options that could be aggregated to eventually become what data visualization will be in the long term. But don't expect that for at least a few more years.

Data have been represented in a visual way for centuries; in fact, according to a report written by Michael Friendly and Daniel Denis at the University of Canada, published on math.yorku.ca, early maps were found carved in stone dating back to around 6200 B.C. and the first known graphical representation of data was recorded around 950 A.D. But it wasn't until the end of the 17th century that elements of true visual thinking were seen. About 100 years' later bar charts were used to represent economic data. Most statistical graphics seen today were developed in the first half of the 19th century; the most advanced at the time being a three-dimensional graphic. According to the report, graphic visualization lost popularity in the early part of the twentieth century in light of numerous new scientific theories and further progress wasn't made until computers became more an integral part of data visualization in the latter part of the 20th century.

New technology then gave rise to data manipulation which allowed visualization to become animated and interactive. According to an article on eric-blue.com, in the early 21st century, the idea of representing data in an aesthetically pleasing way was termed, "Dataesthetics" or "Info-aesthetics". Data visualization had found its second utility and the trend was being adopted in a variety of different ways by businesses and organizations across the globe. As described on dataesthetic.org, "The primacy of information in all aspects of life requires a new understanding of aesthetic values." In essence, new markets could be explored if data was made to look attractive and inviting.

The old cliché, "A picture is worth a thousand words," (first seen in a newspaper article in 1911) has true meaning when, as noted by Javier de la Torre in his article on Data Visualization, 80 percent of our brain is dedicated to visual thinking and written language originated from drawing and sketching. However, visualization requires the capture and analysis of relevant data. According to business intelligence research by the Aberdeen Group reported in the November blog post on spotfire.tibco.com, "When business users can visualize information, they're able to process it more effectively and make faster and better decisions."

Form and function are important parts of data visualization. As noted on dataesthetic.org, "Modular design is efficient, taking less time to deliver, or reserving more time to address aesthetic balance."

David McCandless, a former journalist, described the beauty of data visualization in a clip on youtube.com as a way to represent a large amount of information in a small space. He believes, "Data is the new soil," because of the fertile creative medium required to be effective. He loves the way different shapes, sizes, pictures and colors can be used to represent figures and how, when converted into an interactive app, the data comes alive. He described how technology allows filters to be used to generate specific relationships and how updates can easily be made by changing data in spreadsheets.

Mapping and geolocation have become an important part of data visualization because, as noted by Jorge Garcia in a post on blog.mindjet.com, "Location is a basic criterion for doing business." Garcia quoted a result from a Pitney Bowes white paper that found, "Today, more than 80 percent of all data maintained by an organization has a location component." He explained that handling maps and drilling down data based on a specific region leads to a richer data visualization experience, especially if the data is refreshed when the location is changed. He also described other developments like the use of data mash-up techniques for collecting both structured and unstructured data and integrating it into a single space for analysis. This process enhances any presentation and improves interactivity.

But, as stated by McCandless, absolute figures are not true and can be misinterpreted, therefore you need relative figures connected to other data for true representation. Simple pie charts are no longer enough. As one of the industry-renowned data visualization experts, Edward Tufte, was quoted in the November blog post on spotfire.tibco.com, "The world is complex, dynamic, multidimensional; the paper is static, flat. How are we to represent the rich visual world of experience and measurement on mere flatland?"

Not only does data visualization have to be dynamic, but as described on dataesthetic.org, "Information density is so great that individuals cannot possibly manage it in any direct, unmediated manner." Data drives all functionality; therefore delivering the most information in the shortest amount of time is a necessity for any provider. And because interpretation of visual data is variable, simplicity is paramount. Mobile technology has enabled information workers to access and interpret data wherever they are but, as noted by Garcia, "Going mobile presents a challenge for BI (Business Intelligence) in terms of securing data at all stages of the analytic process, primarily for data transmission and device access." Providers also need to rely on adoption of a certain type of mobile device for a desirable outcome.

Text and scientific reports can be even harder to analyze but new innovation in data visualization is making this process more manageable. According to an article in Scientific American quoted in the October blog post on spotfire.tibco.com blog,

"Building a hypothesis generator sounds like a sea change that could open up doors in science that no one has even considered." This will not be easy because text is always open to a variety of interpretations. Jeffrey Heer, a computer science professor at Stanford University, was quoted in the same blog: "It is vital that visualizations support interactive exploration and verification, so that one can not only uncover new hypotheses but begin the process of assessing their credibility."

Even though companies like Google, IBM and GE have jumped deeply into the data visualization game, supply has already exceeded demand and competition has weakened the trend. In this latent form, otherwise known as trend stage six, data visualization will likely remain until something happens to stabilize the trend in preparation for the long haul. Growth will still occur as we increase our understanding of the world in which we live and data visualization will be better, more creative and profound. As Hans Rosling, a professor of global health at Sweden's Karolinska Institute, concluded in his four-minute clip on youtube.com, "Without statistics we are cast adrift on an ocean of confusion, but armed with stats we can take control of our lives, hold out our rulers and see the world as it really is."

To make the most of this stage six trend, consider the following. Data visualization is a stage six trend. That is, it is retooling itself for the long haul. Data visualization will stay in stage six longer than most. This is due to the fact that there is no one size fits all visualization that works for everyone. The future of visualization may be a common process, instead of a common picture. I would not waste time or effort on visualization right now. Work with what you have and upgrade as new things become available but I would not invest heavily in this area for a few years.It will be years before data visualization enters stage seven.. as many as twenty but at least five to ten.

Example: Private Incubators - Acting on This Stage Six Trend

Incubators are a trend in stage six; that is, they are retooling for longevity. Incubators have enjoyed a long run over several decades rolling casually through the first five stages. Now, they are falling out of favor in their biggest pullback yet as the business community at large tries to figure out what incubators will look like for the long haul. The market was pretty much saturated by the middle of the last decade. Since then, some incubators have dropped out of the market and, during the Great Recession, funding became increasingly difficult to secure. Private incubators...that is, those attached to investors or venture capital firms, are increasing in popularity and profitability and may shape up to be the long term form that incubators everywhere have been seeking. In this example, we highlight the rise and fall of the incubator concept and the private capital-attached incubators that are setting the stage for the future of business incubation to come.

Business incubators have been providing much needed support for fledgling businesses since the 1950s and have morphed into different forms as business needs have changed. Early model private incubators just provided office space and onsite support for up to five years. Meanwhile, universities provided, and continue to provide, a free service to students, educators and grant-aided graduates for a limited period. Toward the end of the 20th century, niche market incubators developed to cater for specific business needs and offered specific equipment and specialized services in return for a percentage of equity.

As technology evolved, the need for speed became apparent as innovators hurtled into a new era. According to J. J. Coleo on forbes.com, "A new breed of incubator, catering mainly to technology types, is springing up all over the country." Besides the basic office services, these accelerator programs offered expert mentors, legal counsel and sometimes seed money in exchange for a percentage stake in the business. These incubator programs are usually offered for three months and are an intense learning curve. As Coleo noted, "Most incubator programs culminate in one fateful day — Demo Day — when the entrepreneurs pitch their companies to a roomful of investors."

And, although funding may be desirable, money is not always the most important resource for a start-up. Jeff Crown of Lycos Labs said in an article on hbswk.hbs.edu, "Experience and services — and connections ("we're probably one degree of separation away from anybody who's anybody on the Internet") are what it takes to get a business going." Also, according to long-time techie, Jeff Bone, in an article on capitalexploits.at, "The trend of late has seemed to be towards smaller, faster-iterating, and bootstrapped or minimally-seeded teams." Today, the number of incubators in the

U.S. has leveled off at around 1250 with only a small percentage in the private sector. Verne Kopytoff noted in the CEO Guide to Business Incubators on businessweek.com, "The vast majority of incubators—93 percent—are operated by nonprofits, according to the National Business Incubation Association. Academic institutions such as universities, economic development organizations, and government agencies are the biggest sponsors." Young entrepreneurs would be wise to max out their time with educational incubators. As one contributor said on blogs.forbes.com, "Stop thinking of college as extended high school and instead think of it as your first business incubator." After all, college students have youth and time on their side and the ability to function well while broke. The biggest advantage is that students have access to mentors and can cultivate a loyal user base that can be used later for leverage with any fledgling company.

Besides, it can be tough in the real world. With a limited pool of available private incubators, competition for access to the best accelerator programs has been likened to securing a place at an Ivy League university. As Kopytoff wrote, "Being accepted into the most prestigious accelerators is like a stamp of approval and significantly lifts a company's chances of getting more funding down the road from venture capitalists." In fact, according to Coleo, "Your odds of getting a bid to Harvard Business School are about three times greater than nabbing a spot in a premium incubator." For this reason, many young people are shunning business school in favor of starting a business through an incubator program.

Success depends on finding the right incubator program; some have very general criteria for acceptance, whereas others are more specialist. Accelerators are usually led by or affiliated with an investment firm. Crown said, "Companies are brought together in an "econet," functioning as "atomic units [that] do only one thing and do it well." He believes that with venture capitalists there is less synergy between partner firms whereas with incubators there is a greater drive to help create something.

Incubators may have a swaddling effect on new businesses, but there are risks. As David Newton noted in his article on entrepreneur.com, "A business incubator is itself an entrepreneurial venture." Investors pool funds to provide office space and resources for businesses and most offer seed funding; revenue is generated from rental or equity stakes. Because of their vested interest, incubator owners often delve deeply into individual business operations in exchange for support. Newton added, "The irony is that many of those benefits can also be reasons not to do capital funding through an incubator. The incubator staff and management team might actually end up being more of a distraction to you. There could be various forms of micromanaging."

Sometimes funds are provided up front; other times, businesses pitch for funding after a period of incubation. Bone noted, "Larger venture funds generally have little time to vet and actually understand the vision and business of a really early-stage company." And too much cash up front in inexperienced hands can cause businesses to grow and burn out too quickly.

Peter Relan, founder of YouWeb incubator, wrote on techcrunch.com that he believed 90 percent of incubators and accelerators would fail in today's market. His reasoning was based on the rule of thumb that nine out of ten start-ups fail. He believes that too many companies with too little mentorship saturate markets with nothing new and claims that many entrepreneurs forget that success involves the solving of compelling problems. He noted, "Many start-ups are just features. They are not products, let alone businesses." Many start-ups don't find sufficient traction within the incubation period—Relan's answer is to kill the idea rather than kill the company, because good innovators will come up with more ideas. Kopytoff believes that business incubators are on the rise, especially those in specific niches, but success rates are difficult to measure. Lack of data collection and difficulty comparing like with like were cited as primary reasons by the authors of an article on yourcapitaledge.com; however, they concluded that incubated firms outperform their peers in terms of employment and sales growth, but tend to fail sooner.

Bone recommended looking for "Smart" money from investors who know your business and can concentrate expertise in your area to maximize their investment and your success. He suggested that micro-funding (miniature private placements, possibly with some uniform and legally-acceptable structure) via equity sales may be on the horizon. To improve your chances of success, Relan advised scrutinizing incubator business models. He said, "There may be hundreds of incubators, but business models are much harder to come by." He added, "Incubators with the best exits and

IPOs under their belts will have the best shot." As for people forgoing business school in favor of starting a business, Relan observed, "We are creating a new education system, one where relevant real-world experience has begun to trump degrees." However, while many companies seek out incubators as a means of reducing the risk of their new venture, they should be cautious that even within an incubator, risk never quite disappears.

To turn this stage six trend into an advantage for your organization, consider the following. Business incubators are a stage six trend. Having enjoyed several decades of evolution and growth, they have pulled back to retool for longevity. Incubators will reach stage seven in the next couple of years. Private incubators are the stage seven version of this trend. The potent combination of available capital, advice and incubation services keep founders focused on growth and significantly increase success rates. Venture firms and investors should add incubation to current efforts. It is a simple add and one that stands to more than double successful exits. Now is the time to act on private business incubators. No matter if you are an investor, a business founder, or just a business junkie, this is the time to get involved. I am personally putting a significant amount of time and effort into private incubators, and I recommend taking the opportunities that arrive for your business in this area.

Conclusions

The future of efforts for this trend in stage six seems really uncertain, as it suffers the largest setback of its existence. At this stage, the trend and those involved with it, must figure out what it will look like long term. They must retool for longevity. If they can, stage 7 will be wonderful, indeed.

Stage 7 - Longevity

Overview

Stage 7, Longevity, is where trends, and the businesses involved with them, achieve long term success. In this stage, company stability and the careers they have fostered seem very solid indeed. And at last, they are. To get to this stage, trends, and the businesses associated with them have had to do some soul searching. They have had to thing hard about what they will be for the long haul. Years and decades from now, what will their brands, products and processes be to the customers they serve? They have found the answer, and the public agreed.

Example - Sustainability

Sustainability

Sustainability is a trend in stage seven and has been there for a long time; since before the data we have. Notice how the level of interest is sustained (pun intended!). It takes dips here and there but is basically always level. This is about where you can expect it to stay. That is important in that, you should not expect MORE interest in sustainability over time. You should also not expect LESS. This caps your market for businesses based on sustainability, but it should have a good long run.

Example - Chocolate

Chocolate

Yes, chocolate is a trend in stage seven. This is another great example of a trend that has found significant longevity and will for the foreseeable future. You are probably saying, "Of course! Everyone loves chocolate!" and that is precisely my point. It is so pervasive that it does not have to work very hard at all to keep its popularity.

Example - Business Advisors

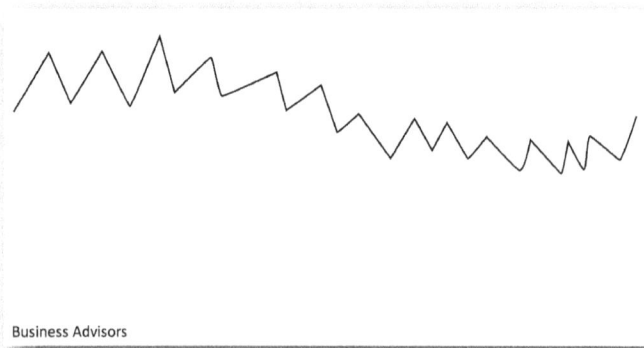

Business Advisors

Yet another great example of a trend long in stage seven, is Business Advisors. In contrast to Business Incubators, this trend is solidly in stage seven and should have a good long run into the future.

Example - Social Media

Social Media has been through it all: stage one to stage seven, all in the last 8 years. It was a fast and bumpy ride but this trend is now in stage seven. As a result, it has spawned other trends like digital marketing.

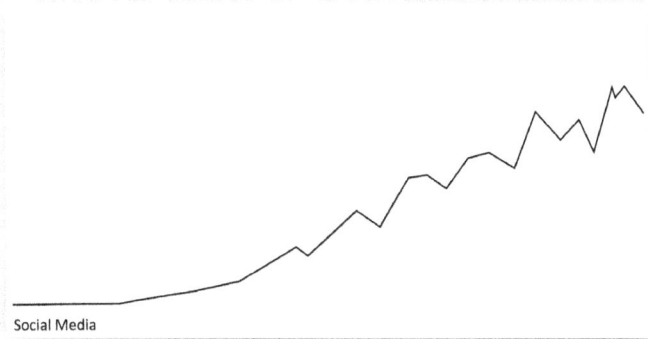

Social Media

Example - Digital Marketing

Digital Marketing

Digital marketing developed right along with social media... slightly thereafter in each stage. It was Social media's first utility and the thing that sparked social media into stage three. Digital marketing, however, is a trend unto itself; and one that has successfully reached stage seven.

What you see now, is basically what you are going to get for many years to come. On the bright side, it is now stable. If your business has not yet begun digital marketing efforts, you are behind the curve. Stop being afraid, and get in there.

Example - Samsung, Apple and LinkedIn

Social media, smartphones and other trends sparked the evolution of many companies. Among them are Samsung, Apple and LinkedIn. Let's take a look at each of these, now stage seven trends.

Samsung

Samsung had a reasonably easy time traversing the seven stages, mostly over the last eight years. Apple, on the other hand, did not have nearly as easy of a time as most people tend to think.

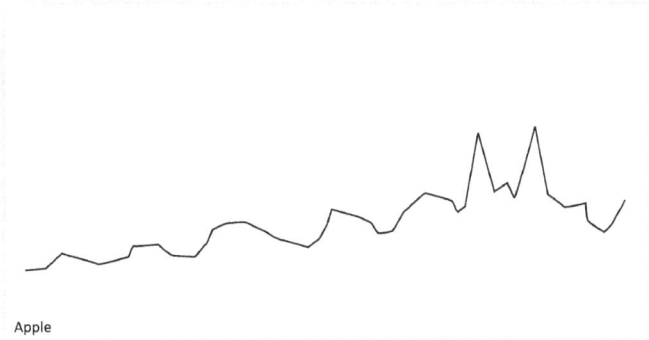

Apple

Stage five was repeated twice, and stage six was particularly painful. Having come through stage six, however, Apple is now beginning stage seven. My bet is that they will remain in their current incarnation for at least another decade without major problems and with a slow growth perspective. In other words, they will start acting more like a "big company."

LinkedIn

LinkedIn is a great case study as it is what we call a supertrend. It has traversed the seven stages, coming recently into stage seven, with unreal ease. They pulled off this feat of business excellence by anticipating downturns and pushing into each growth stage as fast as they could.

Example: Google - Learning From This Stage Seven Supertrend

If you're a technology expert or just a self-confessed geek then the chances are you would aspire to work for Google, a technology company that seems to be more than a fleeting trend. The large majority of all trends go through seven distinct stages of evolution on their way to the coveted stage seven—longevity. Google is no exception. However, as we have noticed, some trends have more painful pullback stages (stages 2, 4 and the dreaded 6) than others. Google has managed to nearly avoid these stages altogether by minimizing them and smoothing them out, earning Google a place among the rare and few known as the supertrends.

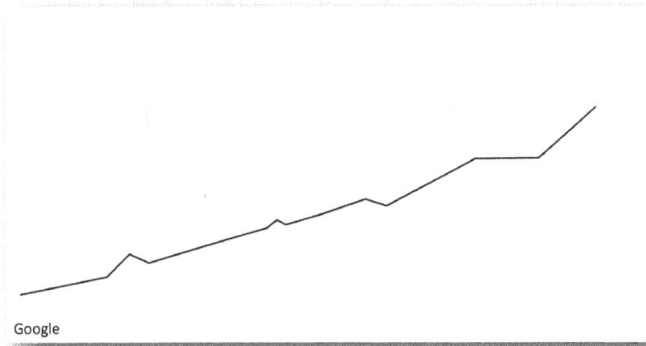

Google

Some people may think that Google just got lucky —right time and right place; but in reality, as noted on ventureblog.com, "Google's success isn't rocket science, it's just good old fashioned company building." This blogger believed Google's success came from the following factors: the founders had a passion for technology and were able to create an innovative business model; the brand may or may not have arisen intentionally, but is now recognized worldwide and Google's focus has always been on the user experience. In this topic, we explore further how Google managed to become a supertrend and what we can all learn from their journey into longevity.

Google's journey began in 1995 when Larry Page met Sergey Brin at Stanford. According to the company's history on google.com, in 1996, Page and Brin worked together on a search engine they named "BackRub" which operated for a year. In 1997, they registered the domain, Google.com; the name was a play on the mathematical term, "googol", which means the numeral 1 followed by 100 zeros. This geek-like terminology represented Page and Brin's mission to organize a vast amount of information on the Web.

In late 1998, with financial investment from Sun co-founder, Andy Bechtolsheim, Google filed for incorporation in California. Working out of a friend's garage, they hired their first employee; within six months, they had to move to bigger premises to accommodate the eight employees that worked for them. With more venture capital the following year, Google expanded rapidly, offered 15 different languages and launched Google AdWords.

2001 was the year Google hired CEO, Eric Schmidt, and Page and Brin were named

Presidents of products and technology. Thereafter, Google introduced numerous different products and concepts; some winners including Google Earth, Gmail and Google Maps and some losers like the social network, Orkut. Google also launched SMS so that people could send text searches from mobile devices.

Google Apps for Your Domain were first introduced in August 2006, shortly followed by the Premier Edition that brought cloud computing to businesses. It's worth noting that in January 2007, "Fortune" announced its annual list of Best Companies to Work For and Google was #1. Google has since won this title three more times and attributes it to this: "Being able to create a company culture where employees are empowered to do cool things that matter."

Despite the Google brand receiving such praise, it never stopped trying to improve itself. In the early years, according to Adam Bryant's article in nytimes.com, Google's approach to management was simple: "Leave people alone. Let the engineers do their stuff. If they become stuck, they'll ask their bosses, whose deep technical expertise propelled them into management in the first place," but this didn't work—"They wanted to build better bosses." This led to Google's People Analytics' teams studying management behavior to develop "The Eight Habits of Highly Effective Google Managers." The results were not startling, as Bryant wrote that it was as if Google was trying to reinvent the wheel, but noted, "Google generally prefers, for better or worse, to build its own wheels."

Not surprisingly, the study found that employees wanted managers to spend more one-on-one time with them and take an interest in their lives and that good managers did not have to be technical experts. The "Eight Habits" were simpler than the numerous rules managers were formerly expected to learn and follow. Bryant likened the ability to keep all those rules in your head to the cliché about improving your golf: "Paralysis by analysis."

Despite Google's study seeming like an exercise in futility, Bryant wrote, "H.R. has long run on gut instincts more than hard data. But a growing number of companies are trying to apply a data-driven approach to the unpredictable world of human interactions." Hiring decisions are therefore made by a group at Google. Laszlo Bock, V.P. of People Operations (H.R.) said in Bryant's article, "We do everything to minimize the authority and power of the manager in making a hiring decision." Employee satisfaction and successful management are a huge part of Google's success and form the backbone of Google's culture. Bock added, "The starting point was that our best managers have teams that perform better, are retained better, are happier—they do everything better."

Even though Google works hard to keep its employees happy, it still suffers from employee turnover and although thousands of people apply to work at the Googleplex every week, loyalty is important to Google. As noted by Zach Bulygo on blog.kissimetrics.com, "When you can retain your employees, it means less time and money spent recruiting." Google has lost hundreds of employees to Facebook and was losing new mothers until H.R stepped in and adjusted the leave and benefits available to them. However, "flexibility is expensive," noted fastcompany.com.

Success often arises from failure. Fastcompany.com wrote, "One big factor is the company's willingness to fail." However, "Good failures also are fast. Fail...but fail early," is their mantra. It's no secret that Google didn't make any money from its Web search service in the first 18 months of operation. According to an article in businessweek.com, "Google didn't make money until it started auctioning ads that appear alongside the search results." Google invented a unique auction method for AdWords that attributed to its success. Despite Yahoo adopting similar features, the article in businessweek.com noted that Google still earned more revenue per ad impression than Yahoo. The secret to Google amassing $9.7 billion in ad revenues according to Panos Mourdoukoutas on forbes.com is innovation, leadership and collective entrepreneurship.

Google has experimented with numerous innovations over the years and many experiments were shut down. Bryant noted, "Google clearly hopes to recapture some of the nimbleness and innovative spirit of its early years." It now intends to put more focus on fewer products and speed up the transition to the marketplace. Page was quoted on blog.kissimetrics.com saying, "As companies get bigger, it tends to take longer to make decisions." He wants people to use technology to make their lives better and added, "At Google we're attacking maybe 0.1 percent of that space. And all the tech companies combined are only at like 1 percent. That means there's 99 percent virgin territory."

Obviously, Google employees have the technological ability and are innovative, but they are also highly focused on the user experience. Fastcompany.com noted, "Google understands that its two most important assets are the attention and trust of its users." Google's personal quote, according to Abhisheck Sharma: "Give users what they want when they want it," and their unofficial slogan, "Don't be evil," reflect a mission with a good purpose. According to Mourdoukoutas, "The bottom line: Google isn't just a technology innovator. It is a business model innovator."

To learn from this supertrend, consider the following. Google's supertrend example is one to follow. They are a great example of how to smooth out your downturns and push forward into growth. Google is a stage seven super trend. That is, they barely felt any pain from stages two, four and six. Google anticipates downturns and utilities. That is how they manage to stay on track. Google turned stage six into no big deal. Whereas, for most, it is the most painful time in the business. Anticipate and prepare to turn your company into a super trend. You can do it! All it takes is the right kind of planning.

Conclusions

In this stage, the trend is now here to stay and will likely begin to spawn new trends that will start the cycle all over again. This stability is a sandbox for new cottage industries, new trends, and new businesses. In short, stage seven is where trends, and the businesses associated with them can breath a bit more easily.

Which leads to the question of what stage is right for whom? Are you a startup junkie who revels in stage one? Are you the stable type who prefers stage seven? An investor who likes stage five?

Making the right move at the right stage is where the magic happens.

Making Your Move

For each trend stage, you have to deal with the stage you are in, and you have to prepare for the next one. In this topic, we explore each of the seven trend stages in turn and give you what you need to know to handle and prepare at each and every one for maximum advantage.

Previously, we discussed the seven stages that the large majority of trends go through. We learned that the overwhelming majority of trends follow the same path of launch, growth and change. The development of each can be tracked, and to a great extent, anticipated. We also saw that all trends are MUTs... Momentum, Utility and Technology must all be in place to make them happen, and to push them to the next stage. The opportunity must exist for the technology, momentum, and utility to all come together in a simple and powerful way. If it does, you have a trend in the making. That trend will then proceed through seven distinct stages: first try, getting real, first utility, limitations, second utility, the competitive tidal wave, and at last longevity.

Knowing the right move to make at each stage is the key to creating advantage for yourself, your investors, your career and ultimately your bottom line. Let's take each stage in turn.

Stage 1, First Try, is when the first prototypes of the technology, business model, industry, service, etc are attempted. The trend has not yet found its first real utility in this stage; instead, it is just trying some things out.

In this stage, startup junkies should get involved. Investors, unless you are specifically about the startup stage, might want to steer clear and keep these companies on your radar. This stage is specifically the domain of the startup, the skunkworks inventor, and the brave at heart.

Stage 2, Getting Real, is when public interest pulls back from this trend. That bit of experimentation in stage one was fun, but we have real businesses to run here. Momentum wanes, technology may stall out or have trouble moving forward, and the first real utility is still forming.

In this stage, your best move is figure out what the first real utility will be. Get ahead of the next stage.

Develop the product that will launch stage three; become a part of that company, and get involved, in a tentative sense. Wait for the momentum, utility and technology to come together and prepare.

Stage 3, First Utility, is where we see the first real, polished and tested products, services, and monetization of a trend. Momentum picks up significantly as hype, excitement and discussion about this new useful thing for immediate return on investment ripples through the business world.

In this stage, you best move is to not be drawn too far into the hype. Jumping on board for your career, investments and other interests is a great thing to do, but don't fool yourself that stage four will never happen. Prepare to shorten stage four by anticipating the second utility that will launch stage five's growth.

Stage 4, Limitations, is where businesses acting on this trend must get clever. Interest, and possibly revenues at this stage have pulled back yet again. Momentum stalls as headlines suggest that maybe this trend is past its peak and not the great thing we all thought it might be.

At this stage, finding the second real utility is key. It is the only thing that will get you out of the slump and back into growth. Create the products and efforts that will launch the second utility and get out of this stage as fast as you can.

Stage 5, Second Utility, is where we see the largest amount of solid business growth for any given trend. Momentum picks back up as headlines and individuals return to their original excitement. Technology is well in hand to make it happen, and businesses acting on this trend seem to really be solidifying their place in the world.

In this stage, you best move is to get involved in any way you can. Take a job, make an investment, etc. At this point, most companies involved in this trend are entering growth phases and lower mid-market status. It is an investor's dream and the beginnings of a great career move. At the same time, you need to be anticipating stage six, and preparing to make it as short as possible by preparing for longevity.

Stage 6, The Competitive Tidal Wave, is where we see giants fall (or so it would seem). The future of efforts for this trend seems really uncertain, as it suffers the largest setback of its existence.

At this stage, the trend and those involved with it, must figure out what it will look like long term. They must retool for longevity. This is the hardest undertaking because it requires the most social permission, that is, momentum.

Stage 7, Longevity, is where trends, and the businesses involved with them, achieve long term success. In this stage, company stability and the careers they have fostered seem very solid indeed.

In this stage, you best move depends on your perspective. For most venture firms, now is a great time to exit, if you have not already. For investment houses, the right move is usually to get in here and stay in long term. For careers made in this trend, enjoy your newfound glory. And for those looking for career stability, these are the trends to focus on.

No matter the stage, there is advantage to be found. Remember the following:

- Trend stage one is for startup junkies only. Jump in if you dare.

- Trend stages two and four can be shortened. They can, in some cases be avoided entirely. We will discuss that in a later section when we study Google.

- Trend stages three and five offer real growth. This is where careers are made and venture firms make money.

- Trend stage six cannot be avoided. But it can be shortened by planning ahead. This is the stage to be the hero, or fail miserably.

- Lastly, trend stage seven is where stability is found. Long term investment, stable careers and stable companies live here.

Convergence and Divergence

Trends do not act or evolve in a vacuum unto themselves. They affect each other, accelerate each other, enable, disable and slow each other down. For example, the evolution of a technology trend can accelerate or slow down the evolution of a business model trend based on that technology.

When trends converge, a powerful thing happens to boost the evolution of a larger trend, and of each trend individually. When trends diverge, that is, when they work against each other, an equally undeniable force slows them all down and can halt progress entirely. In this topic, we explore why and how trends converge and diverge, what happens next and what you need to do to create advantage from either side.

Convergence speeds things up. Divergence slows things down. Let's start with convergence. Trend convergence is when the evolution of one trend aids the evolution of another. They have an additive effect on each other. Sometimes they multiply each other; sometimes the effect is nearly exponential (for my mathematical friends out there).

Trends have three critical components: Momentum, Utility and Technology. When trends converge and accelerate each other, we usually find that one of them is more heavily steeped in one of these areas, while the other is focused on another of these three. For example, a trend that is heavily focused on momentum can accelerate a technology focused trend by accelerating the social permission to proceed.

For example, Freelancing is a trend that is heavy on momentum and utility, but whose evolution was slowed by lack of technology for many years. Mobile technologies, as they evolved, accelerated freelancing by rapidly pushing forward the technology component needed; even to the point that the technology has outpaced the freelancers, whose momentum and utility will continue to evolve quickly as a result. In other words, mobile technologies emerged as a trend that ultimately accelerated the trend of freelancing... this is trend convergence.

The WHY and HOW of trend convergence (and divergence) all comes down to these three things:

148

Momentum, Utility and Technology. If a trend slows or accelerates one of these facets for another trend, the effect can be significant.

Let's take a look at divergence now. Divergence of trends is just the opposite of convergence - it happens when the evolution of one trend slows or prevents the evolution of another.

For example, a combination of privacy concerns (a trend) and social momentum towards simplicity, is slowing down the evolution of location-based marketing. It is not preventing the evolution of location-based marketing. In fact, the corporate-based momentum is so strong that this trend will most certainly move forward. Backlash, however, from a concerned public who does not want to be surveilled, is slowing things down.

Such divergence means that the location-based marketing trend will take longer in each stage and have a harder time in each pullback stage (2, 4, and 6). Retooling for longevity will be particularly difficult and even more so as long as governments and trusted organizations are getting in trouble with the public over what they see as development of a surveillance state.

Trend convergence and divergence is powerful indeed. It can stall out trends, accelerate them, and otherwise regulate the timing of their run through the seven stages of trend evolution. It pays to be aware not only of the trends that affect your business and career, but of the trends that in turn affect the trends.

Once aware, the big question is what to do about it. Let's suppose you have invested your time, effort and possibly money in a particular business. Look hard at the industry you have chosen. Categorize and study the big three factors: Momentum, Utility and Technology. Catalog the major trends that are driving your business and industry and understand what stage they are currently in, and approximate timing for stages to come.

Understanding which stage the major trends are in is only the first step. For each of those trends, you need to catalog the trends that converge or diverge with them. The major trends that form the basis of your industry or business are susceptible to this convergence and divergence; and your business is susceptible just the same. By understanding the trends that affect the trends; you put yourself in a position to better predict the timing and evolution of the major trends in your industry. If timing is everything, this larger picture will put your in a position to make much smarter decisions and position your business ahead of the competition who remains unaware.

Trend convergence and divergence is best understood through example. What follows are nine examples of trend convergence and divergence from the last few years.

Example: Your Company IS The Product - Converging Trends Affecting The Design of Your Business (2012)

More so, your company itself is becoming the base product that you sell. If that product is weak, so too will be your sales. The company-product is scrutinized more and more by shareholders, customers who place importance on brand idea, and those who boost your business like incubators and boards of advisors. In this article, we explore how the brand itself is increasingly important as your number one product, what it means for your business going forward and what to do about it.

Trends evolve and sometimes trends converge. When trends converge, they may slow each other down, or accelerate each other. When two trends are at odds, the result can be stagnation for both. When two or more trends are pushing in similar directions, however, the result can be vary fast evolution of each trend involved. At a minimum, it is a boost for at least one of the trends. There are four trends all pushing your brand to become more important than your products. These are: brand idea, boards of advisors, incubators, and shareholder activism. Having so many trends all pushing in the same direction is causing this evolution of the company as product to happen much faster than it might naturally.

Brand idea, covered previously, is that all important emotion evoked by the mere mention of your brand. That feeling you give customers is becoming more important than the product you deliver. The product has to live up to it, but the base foundation of a great brand idea is enough to get you through even the toughest times and product failures. The importance of brand idea is accelerated by other trends such as boards of advisors, incubators and shareholder activism. Each of these trends places increasing emphasis on the brand instead of on individual products offered.

Boards of advisors are critical to your business success. Attracting top advisors can be the key to unlocking strategic partnerships, avoiding the need to reinvent the wheel and generally save you lots of time, effort and money. The best advisors are drawn to strong brands. Advising your company looks good on their résumé only is your brand itself looks good. So attracting the best advisors becomes a matter of strong brand, and less a matter of product offering. It is not that the products are irrelevant, but that it is less important than the strong base brand.

Incubators come in all varieties, including public and private. While public incubators are open to everyone, private incubators are often extensions of angel or venture investors. These private incubators exist to give chosen companies the best possible chance of success. So how do you become chosen? It starts with... You guessed it... A strong brand. Preferably one with a neat product idea. But product is secondary to brand. This is year another boost to the brand as product in and of itself.

Shareholder activism is perhaps the most powerful force accelerating the emergence of your brand itself as your chief product. Shareholder activism, covered previously, is a seemingly simple trend wherein your shareholders want to have a say... In everything... Right down to corporate governance, executive salaries and corporate culture. Active shareholders are driven to invest not by the products you offer but by the by the brand you portray.

Each of these individual trends are converging to accelerate each other toward the end state of your products being secondary to your brand when it comes to the ultimate success of your business. With this much force behind the move, it is likely to become even more prevalent in the coming years.

To turn this trend into an advantage for your business, consider the following. Trends are converging to make your brand the product. Brand idea, boards of advisors, incubators and shareholder activism all push your brand to be your top product. Your brand-product attracts advisors and incubators. Without a strong brand, these resources will not be available to you. Shareholders demand brand over product. They back the brand or tear it down, often without regard to specific products. Shore up your brand before anything else. Your brand is your base product so make sure it is strong and accepted by the market before your worry about specific products. Use products to boost the brand. Instead of the other way around, use your product offerings to boost your brand further.

Example: Living in the Swarm — Converging Trends Redefining the Marketplace (2011)

Several trends are converging to change the nature and operation of your marketplace. It used to be very compartmentalized like a bento box: there was you, your competition, and the mass of people known as your customers. But the lines have become blurred...your competition may be your customer, your customer may be your competition, and you may be a bit of both to yourself. The marketplace has taken on a swarm-like feel that you now must operate within. This article will examine the changing market place and the use of social media for competitive intelligence to uncover your real competition.

Knowing your market is one thing, but knowing your competitors is another and once again, technology and social media are responsible for making the marketplace more accessible to a wider range of producers. Fast-paced technology has made it easier and cheaper for more people to create similar products or services and social media has created a wide open platform for ideas and trends to be voiced, opinions to be expressed and word to get out in general. As noted in an earlier Trend POV article about Direct to Profit, "One must look at the signs of the times…and realize that new technology and market platforms have provided producers with a lot more avenues to get their products onto the marketplace."

Producers will always be driven by profit and the idea of cutting out the middle man is not new. If businesses can create their own distribution methods and use social media to market directly to the consumer, they can retrieve more profit. Davy Knowles of Back Door Slam said of the music industry's return to direct sales, "These new distribution avenues (such as the Internet) bring the artist closer to the consumer again." Using many of the characteristics that companies rely on for repeat business—loyalty, familiarity, and action, "They're actually building a stronger fan base by relying on distribution themselves," said Knowles. Consumers are now much more involved in grass roots market decisions. For example, in the music industry, digitalization has meant that for some time now customers have been able to choose to buy a selection of songs from an album instead of the whole album or just one single.

In an attempt to get one up on competitors, many businesses that produce directly for the customer have been drawn toward creating a market for more specialized, custom-made products. In Trend POV's article about Using Individualization for Advantage, it was seen that mass customization has been used to meet diverse customer needs but the choices had to be simple and easy to implement. Customization was deemed advantageous for smaller businesses as they could adapt easily, but bigger companies would find it difficult and expensive to react quickly to such specificity.

According to John Paul Titlow on readwriteweb.com, "Previously, mass customization faced several obstacles to really becoming a viable option for businesses. Incomplete implementations, cost overruns and primitive digital interfaces all made it difficult for mass customization to work." Titlow believes that now technology is more affordable and has become more advanced, businesses are able to build sophisticated, yet easy-to-use interfaces (configurators) from which consumers can co-create products without the cost and complexity of outside intervention. In other words, the customer has become your competition.

In Trend POV's article about Social Media Driving the Pace of Business, the Trendspotting's 2009 report suggested, "Quality will trump quantity as users are overwhelmed with content." This is a very valid point because consumers may well reach saturation point with information overload, so marketers will have to work harder to isolate competitors and entice customers to buy in. As the article suggested, "Exclusivity may draw potential clients who are currently used to open networkers looking for business anywhere they can get it."

But competition taken in context can be a good wake-up call for business; it prevents complacency from setting in. Businesses need to be considering three types of competition: direct, indirect, and what Rich Harshaw, CEO of Y2 Marketing calls the "dreaded inertia" in his article on businessknohow.com. Direct competition is easy to find because it stares you in the face with every commercial you see promoting the same product or service as your business. Indirect competition comes from businesses selling services or products in fields related to yours; with available technology, these affiliates have the potential to become direct competitors. The "dreaded inertia" competitor is the mass of potential customers who believe they can live perfectly well without your product or service—in other words, the untapped market that directs its energy and spending elsewhere. All of these competitors could easily become your customers in the current socially diverse marketplace.

But, as Trend POV's article about Recognizing your Real Competition points out, "As customers have grown in power, so have their expectations, and their expectations are your real competition." You have to understand your customers' competitive space and realize that if you don't meet their expectations, they will dismiss you in the bat of an eyelid and look elsewhere, many times directly toward the producer. This is what is known as customer-induced competition and has been seen in the banking industry with places like WalMart and Google wanting to open their own financial institutions. As Tom Brzezina was quoted, "If you let a camel's head in the tent, pretty soon the whole camel is in the tent."

The other downside of the increased speed and expectation of this swarm-like trend is that news also travels faster than ever before, especially bad news. As noted in Trend POV's Social Media Driving the Pace of Business, "Each video view, blog view, tweet and post is a part of a larger swarm of conversation that may be for you, against you, or ignoring you." And negativity can be contagious according to a report in eurekalert.com, "Given the strong influence of negative information, marketers may need to expend extra resources to counter-act the effects of negative word of mouth in online chat rooms, blogs and in offline media." Conversely, as Brad Shorr said in his blog, "Negative comments in and of themselves are unlikely in and of themselves to drive business away." So, businesses should turn this to their advantage.

As far as choice goes, businesses should not over-think this element because too much choice will drive customers away in search of easier options. And, although DIY distribution may conjure up multiple dollar signs, Trend POV's Direct to Profit article noted, "Moving to direct distribution has its challenges. It means taking on every function surrounding the product including some you may not be well versed in." Producers also have to be able to react to fraud, leaks and cheaper markets.

In order to remain competitive, companies need to rethink how they conduct competitive analyses of the market that they operate within. Looking at the whole market and considering the real competition in context will prevent future irrelevancy. In Trend POV's article on Mining Social Media for Competitive Intelligence, Renee Johnson said, "It can get complicated and intricate but at the core it is knowing what the strategy, finances, products, services, customers and partners of your business opposition look like." Social Media may be a primary tool, but should not be the only tool. Being where your competition is and being responsive to change are key factors to consider along with the knowledge that your business, regardless of size, is equally transparent to others looking for a competitive edge.

To act on this convergence of trends for a competitive edge, consider the following. Understand the swarm business environment. There is not the tidy separation of employees, competition and customer that there used to be.

Rethink your competition. They may be in house, your customer or your partner but rarely is it so pure as to just be your competition. Rethink your customers. They are not who you think they may be and that definition may change under different circumstances. It may be time to segment in a new way. Rethink your employees. When might they be your competition or your customer or partner? Segment markets differently. Segmenting individuals is no longer relevant. Consider segmenting by circumstance or other factors.

Example: Striking the Balance - Converging Trends Driving Global Networks with Local Implications (2011)

As global alliances emerge in all aspects of business production, partnerships and communications, collaboration is taking place on a massive global scale and a balance must be found that addresses the local and individual nature of each global partner, competitor, market and consumer. Each country, entity and element of our local and global networks must be treated as an individual, whether ally or competitor. This article examines how these trends converge to drive a need to balance local or individual attention to every part of our global efforts while handling the massive scale of entire operations.

As businesses grow, it's natural to assume they will want to expand into markets elsewhere in the world in order to grow their market, but this is not as easy as it may seem at the outset. Cultural differences in different countries have created challenges that businesses have had to address. Many times this has involved tailoring products to suit local preferences in a global market. This process resulted in the term, "glocalization" and subsequently led to reverse innovation. As Immelt, Govindarajan, and Trimble noted in a Trend POV article on Preparing to Balance Localization and Globalization, "To do that, they'd have to develop innovative new products that met the specific needs and budgets of customers in those [local] markets."

Even back in 1999, one of the original globalized markets, Coca-Cola, had to embrace changes to keep up with customer needs. New CEO at the time, Douglas Daft, said in a report on hbswk.hbs.edu, "The world in which we operate has changed dramatically, and we must change to succeed…No one drinks globally. Local people get thirsty and…buy a locally made Coke." He soon realized there was more to globalization than could be dealt with in a geographically modified business model. As noted in the report, "The key strategic challenge was simply to determine how much to adapt the business model—how much to standardize from country to country versus how much to localize to respond to local differences."

Many businesses wanted to go global in an attempt to exploit price differentials, but failed because they did not take localization factors into consideration. Computer manufacturer, Acer, acknowledged, "The logic of exploiting similarities often calls for targeting countries similar to a company's home base, whereas the logic of arbitrage involves exploiting one or more of the differences inherent in distance." Companies like CEMEX and GEMS bundled operations and applied centrally developed learning templates where arbitrage economies were being pursued.

PhD student, Danah Boyd spoke about glocalization at a technology conference in 2006. She said, "When mass media began, people assumed that we would all converge upon one global culture. While the media has had an effect, complete homogenization has not occurred. And it will not." One reason she indicated was that people are a part of multiple cultures comprising religion and nationality, but she also observed there are many sub-cultures that form from identities and communities of practice. She noted that while some cultural values are adopted universally, others are too deeply ingrained and serve to differentiate smaller groups of people from one another.

Networking through technological media has brought people who may be globally diverse closer together but Boyd noted, "How you see the world and how you design or build technology is greatly influenced by the various cultural concepts you hold onto."

In research conducted at the University of Toronto, Barry Wellman determined, "Communities have changed from densely-knit "Little Boxes" (densely-knit, linking people door-to-door) to "Glocalized" networks (sparsely knit but with clusters, linking households both locally and globally) to "Networked Individualism" (sparsely -knit, linking individuals with little regard to space)." He explained that the world now comprises social networks not groups therefore making boundaries more permeable. Virtual global alliances have been formed that have resulted in work effusing beyond a work group's former boundaries creating more informal relationship.

As a result of glocalized connectivity, people are no longer identified as members of a single group; they now switch among multiple networks and use these networks to share resources—which can ultimately result in new business, trade or cooperation. Networked individualism means that people no longer have to be tied to a location to receive information. Mobile technology, according to Wellman means, "The person has become the portal," therefore physical context becomes less important.

But, as with many emerging trends, there are some downsides. At the grass roots level, people live and work in networks and work concurrently on multiple projects all from their computer desks. According to Wellman, "Computer mediated communications supplements, arranges and amplifies in-person and telephone communications rather than replacing them." In other words, technology has added to people's workload and may result in online overload. Also, with global outreach, businesses have to be acutely aware of cultural differences that, if ignored, may result in online tensions.

Globally, alliances may be great for business communication and resources; after all, everyone needs friends but some, like the one connecting Venezuela, Cuba, China, Russia and Iran, may well be catastrophic for the Western world. So, as the Trend POV article on Balancing Localization and Globalization points out,"If globalization endangers local cultures, is localization also likely to isolate them?"

According to the book titled, World out of balance: navigating global risks to seize competitive advantages by Paul A. Laudicina, "As companies expand abroad, they open themselves up to a world of new risks: political and social upheaval, natural disasters, terrorist attacks and unpredictable labor." Laudicina recommends that businesses need to step outside of their own microscopic world to focus on external risk management because problems frequently arise from government regulation, vague laws, international finance and currency issues, and political and social disturbances.

Meanwhile, the economic gap between rich and poor countries is widening affecting politics, security, society and culture. Consequently, according to an article in chinadaily.com, "The lopsided international economic order has seriously affected the sustainable development of the global economy."

But the internet has expanded trade beyond many people's wildest dreams and has inspired the creation of communities that may never have otherwise formed. Mass collaboration has succeeded in keeping geographically diverse businesses connected although, according to the Trend POV article on The Profit Game, "Processes need to be streamlined and simplified and include a high level of understanding and user friendliness in order for cloud technology to drive transformation and create savings." According to the report on hbswk.hbs.edu, the future of globalization is not certain, but it is possible to apply different strategies to different elements of a business. The author pointed out that businesses may integrate further into the global market once economic conditions improve, but they may also go into reverse because of the economic instability of many countries.

Maybe we should follow the lead of social networks, Craigslist, MySpace and Flickr, where founding members essentially live and breathe the culture they are continuously modifying. As Boyd noted, "Embedded observation allows developers to understand culture. They are doing a form of ethnography, the method used by those seeking to understand culture." And, although millions of the users are not invested in the culture, Boyd believes, "The key here is to diversify the folks behind the scenes to reflect the diversity of your community."

To act on this convergence of trends for a competitive edge, consider the following. Global scale cannot ignore individual needs. As we scale operations, processes and systems, we cannot stop paying attention to the individual employees, competitors and allies that make us who we are. Employees must be treated individually. They have individual talents, potential and motivations. Competitors must be treated individually. They each have their own agendas, plans, and tactics. Allies and partnerships need individual attention. Each has their own agenda, preferences, and resources. Use networks to balance global scale and individual treatment. Computer networks are great but human networks can help you to address individual aspects while handling scale.

Example: Putting On The Breaks - How The Simplicity Backlash May Slow Efforts To Reach Your Team (2011)

Technology evolved so rapidly in the past decade you had to be careful when you blinked in case you missed something, but screen face-time and use of social media may have peaked regardless of innovation; the reason behind this changing trend could be that people have reached saturation point. Just when many businesses have caught up with using social media to track down and interact with customers, those same customers are switching off or hitting delete and saying, "No more." This article looks at how the simplicity backlash may hold back some aspects of evolving media consumption and innovative incentives and how businesses may have to adapt to communicate with employees and customers.

Simplicity may become the new buzz word as people get overwhelmed by technology and over-connectivity. New technology will still evolve and will likely create excitement in fits and starts, but mass consumption of multiple electronic gadgets may slow—or potentially merge. With only a limited number of hours in the day, people will become more selective with their screen time; some may cut back on social media by selecting preferred sites or subscribing to fewer updates. And individuals may consolidate their electronic devices to avoid extra pressure on their time. The upshot of this trend seems to be that companies will have to get more creative—yet again—to get people to notice them.

In Trend POV's Three Screens a Day article earlier this year, we referred to a study conducted by The Pew Research Center that compared people's technology habits from the year, 2000, with those in 2010. All the numbers showed increases: internet usage, cell phone ownership, wireless connectivity, social networking and adult daily usage of the internet; the technology world was blooming!

The Nielsen Three Screen Report from the second quarter of 2009 summed up, "Americans are increasing their overall media consumption, and media multi-tasking is part of the equation." Consumers were able to use televisions, cell phones and the internet simultaneously. Jim O'Hara, President, Media Product Leadership, the Nielsen Company, said, "The entire media universe is expanding so consumers are choosing to add elements to their media experience, rather than to replace them." Figures from Cisco indicated the biggest growth driver was video, "which will lead global mobile traffic to double every year for the foreseeable future." Netbooks, e-readers and tablets were also predicted to quadruple IP usage in the next three or four years according to Marie Kerwin in adage.com.

Meanwhile, many businesses also discovered game-based incentive schemes to reward employees and keep them motivated. Although many of these schemes were deemed successful, they also meant more screen time for the work force. But it's not just at work that people use all this technology; they walk or drive while using cell phones; they surf the net for deals while grocery shopping; they catch up with emails and social media in-between television programs or family activities in the evenings.

Andre Yee reported on bizq.net, "According to Nielsen, users spent significantly more time (approximately five and one half hours) on social network sites in 2009 than the preceding year with Facebook usage outpacing all other sites (six hours). This represents an 82 percent jump in usage time." This frenzy of activity resulted in increased advertising revenue and greater corporate buy-in. He added, "According to emarketer.com, ad spend on social media worldwide will be up 12 percent totaling $2.2 billion. Facebook advertising spend is estimated to grow even faster at 39 percent." This appeared to be great news for skeptical marketers; however, those seeking greater clarity may still be hovering in the wings because quantifying return on investment with internet marketing is still a learning curve for many.

No sooner had these figures been released than things started to change. CBC news reported in Calgary that sign-up rates for social media networking were slowing down. They said, "While networking sites such as Twitter are still growing at lightning speed—the sign-up rate for new users has slowed significantly, according to a recent statistical analysis by RJ Metrics." The company's research suggested that, "While Twitter now has 75 million users, many of them are inactive, one-fourth of twits have no followers and 40 percent of those who signed up for Twitter have yet to send a single tweet."

It's as if the novelty of social networking wore off. University of Calgary communications and culture Professor, Maria Bakardjieva, referred to the

173

bandwagon effect, "Later on they come to realize this whole business is over-rated and they are not getting very much in return." Networks had become crowded; people were suffering from information overload. A recent report on i-policy.org noted, "According to a study by Gartner, Trends in Consumers' Use of Social Media, the trend shows some social media fatigue among early adopters."

Fatigue seems an apt description. According to Spencer Ante, "Slowing and/or declining growth will make it harder to generate sales and profit growth from these sites. That will put more pressure on the advertising programs to deliver results." A blog post on emarketer.com predicted that the current 150 million social media users in the US would only rise to 164.2 million by 2013, an increase of a little over three percent of the total online population. Debra Aho Williamson, emarketer principal analyst said, "You can't rely on the social networks to do your job for you anymore. Rather than let them add net-new bodies for you, you'll need to work harder to segment, locate, engage and convert."

This may seem like stating the obvious, but with more voices to choose from, social network users will become choosier about sites they interact with and how they use their screen time.

According to Trend POV's Simplicity Backlash article, "51 percent of workers spend half their work days managing and processing information rather than using that information to do their jobs." Now, that's a scary statistic that indicates a need for simplification and more streamlined scheduling of time spent with technology. Business executives need to focus their marketing efforts on social networks that will enhance their business brand.

As contributions to social media sites decline, video and blog entries will be fewer and diminishing comments and reviews will make content less reliable. Juan Carlos Perez noted in computerworld.com, "Companies need to find ways to re-engage those U.S. Internet users who have stopped participating on their social media sites." The emarketer.com report recommends a game plan for targeted engagement that helps you pick up a larger share of new markets by being aggressive and effectively blocking out competition by creating and owning new trends. Meanwhile, marketers need to be wary of consumer tolerance (think Facebook and Netflix).

175

An interesting piece of advice was recently given by Jonathan Salem Baskin in an article on cmo.com. He recommended figuring out how to slow down—and then getting your customers to do the same. The result would hopefully be a more meaningful relationship between you, the customer and your brand. He advised marketers to put more time, and therefore more thought, into brand promotion in order to stimulate understanding and recognition that would promote memorable encounters for customers.

According to a recent article on vomo.co.za, there is a firm belief that another massive boom in mobile advertising is likely to take place. Industry leaders, Gartner, predicted that growth in 2011 is likely to be double that in 2010 translating to advertising revenue of $3.3 billion; this could be significant in global industries that will benefit from falling data rates, cheaper handsets and increased consumer demand for goods and services through the internet. And although double-digit growth in social network users may be over, emarketer.com predicted for 2011, "The highest penetration level of all age groups will remain in the 18-to-24 age group, where 90 percent of internet users will use social networks this year."

To act on this convergence of trends for a competitive edge, consider the following. Simplicity backlash may slow motivation trends. Social media integration could be a turn-off for those who are feeling burned out. Simplicity backlash will not stop workforce trends from moving forward. The eventual use of social media integrated motivation and tracking systems will see full maturity, but the backlash may be a bump in the road. Social media integration may adopt later for internal communication. As employees feel burned out, they may push back on internal communications via social media or encroachment of work into personal networks. Do not push social and mobile communications on your workforce. Forcing the issue will make a backlash worse. Offer it as an option instead for faster adoption. Lastly, be patient with workforce objectives. Things will take time, but the backlash is only temporary.

Example: Rule of All - Converging Trends Driving Your Digital Strategies (2011)

In recent years, digital marketing has changed the way businesses seek out and retain customers and has even opened the doors for customers to have a say in how businesses operate. It has driven interaction between providers and consumers in a way that has not only let customers share experiences, but has given them a sense of power that has led to them demanding to be heard and be a part of future product development. This level of interaction is likely to grow into a deeper conversation that includes customers' opinions in many aspects of business. As modern-thinking businesses, you are expected to keep up with the evolving digital marketing world. You need to be able to interact digitally, deliver great apps, engage and involve your customers so that they become a part of your concept in such a way that they tell all their social network friends and keep coming back for more. This article examines the convergence of trends in digital marketing and will help you navigate your way through a marketing minefield.

A timeline detailed on spotlightideas.co.uk recorded that digital marketing first spawned in the early 90s with the introduction of Lycos, the first commercially successful search engine. Banner advertisements were introduced soon after and became a new platform for marketers to attract customers. Next, full text search engines were developed which resulted in search results being ranked by relevancy adding a competitive edge to Web presence.

Web logs and blogging emerged in the late 90s bringing an official classification to opinionated content and giving internet users a legitimate way to openly communicate concerns about products and services while inviting comments and suggestions from followers. Although Yahoo surfaced in 1994, Google took the upper hand when it was founded in 1998. The timeline outlines the arrival of many other popular marketing sites in the millennium decade including Wikipedia, LinkedIn, MySpace, Flickr, Facebook and YouTube indicating how quickly digital marketers had to adapt to constantly changing platforms.

As Web sites proliferated, technology advanced and user interest grew, interactivity became the new buzz word. Users were not only able to choose and view content on demand, but they were able to easily create their own content and share it with others. As noted by Russ Hopkinson in his article on A Brief History of Digital Media, "The Web is moving from a place where people access content…to a place where people access people in an information and content rich environment." Change came rapidly and marketers had to think quickly in order to keep up with consumer demand and avoid loss of customer engagement.

As noted in Trend POV's article on Navigating the Evolving World of Digital Marketing, "Digital marketing has both helped and hurt companies because of the many different marketing tools and mediums available today." Today, there are numerous digital marketing channels that can be used to promote products and services including television, radio, internet, digital billboards, mobile phones and social media marketing, but the underlying marketing principals of pull and push marketing remain the same.

Most marketers develop strategies to push content to their consumers via email newsletters, RSS feeds, apps and social networks because they can target select groups of potentially interested customers; whereas pulled content relies on consumers actively seeking out your particular product or service. As Trend POV pointed out, "Pull activates others organically, which of course cedes control," therefore in reality, pull strategies are generally more effective. But in order to entice your customer, "Your digital marketing must do more than catch their eye. It must inspire to action and interaction." Your message must also be consistent and influential to retain interest. As Adam Singer at TheFutureBuzz.com noted, "There is an inequality of influence on the web held by a minority." He said companies should seek out and partner with influencers.

Influence is not just restricted to the Web, although word of mouth certainly has the ability to spread globally at great speed through the internet, but let's not forget the impact of the honor system—a unique form of marketing that got to the very core of consumerism by using people's conscience to drive sales. As noted in Trend POV's article on The Honor System, "It's not just about price, but convenience." On the one hand, the product is easily accessible to consumers without having to consider the bottom line; but on the other, there is the positive attribute for customers who like to be seen to be doing the right thing for social acceptance. Either way, people like to feel they have influence and the resultant success motivates other businesses to rethink their strategies.

But there is also a disruptive influence created by giving customers control. Consumers now believe they are an integral part of new product development and that product managers should

take heed of every suggestion made. As Daniel Shefer said in his article on Disruptive Customer Demands, "New feature requests are basically like the beginning of a new sales cycle. The request needs to be addressed like an objection."

Suggestions, criticisms and complaints can be a useful wake-up call for businesses but product development should not be totally consumer driven because the costs of making the changes can rapidly spiral out of control. Companies need to find a balance between satisfying customer demand for a particular feature and updating products in a timely manner. It may be that the company needs to review its chosen target market. As noted by Bill Peyton, Principal, IP-Digital in Shefer's article, "If they give the customer what they want, they may continue to fight the next day but will have disrupted, sometimes severely, their own vision and roadmap." In other words, don't let yourself be bullied.

Managing customer demand is not easy. As Ken Faw said in his blog, "We can't manage demand anyway... we can only manage the promises we make and what we deliver with the resources at our disposal." Jason Compton believes it is possible to manage customer expectations by clearly defining the roles of each party. He said in his article, "Customers cannot be expected to honor your expectations and requirements if they aren't aware of them." Many businesses have succeeded in maintaining loyalty from customers by encouraging complaints and anticipating problems. Others learned how important it was to learn from their mistakes, as was noted in customerexpressions.com, "Don't let automation get between the front-line employee and the customer." In essence, keep the human touch.

The relatively new introduction of mobile apps seems to hold the key to the future of digital marketing; products can still be pushed through free apps, but consumers can control what they receive by choosing what to download. More select products and services come at a price, but the customer still has the freedom to choose. According to Trend POV's article, Is There an App for That? "Markets and Markets reported that the global mobile applications market will be worth about $25 billion by 2015, from about $6.8 billion in 2010."

However, marketing through apps still has to provide end user value to retain customer interest. "Users want those apps that interact with their lives." Business apps soon took over consumer apps in the short time since apps were created but, "Mobile apps that provide consumers with value in terms of reference and news have the highest user retention rates of all apps," said Helen Leggatt in Trend POV's article. Apps that make life easier seem most popular so long as they don't require input of hefty amounts of personal data— think more intimate shopping experience with added value. When creating apps, businesses also need to focus on holding customer attention because Pew research has already found a sharp decline in customer use of apps as time passes.

To act on this convergence of trends for a competitive edge, consider the following. Digital is driving interaction. Social, mobile and other digital communications make it easy for your market to interact with you. Interaction is not the end state for digital. That is, it is a means to an end, but only step one. Customers want involvement in every aspect of your business. Products, governance, executive pay and more are all on their minds and they want to have their say. Decide where to draw the line on customer interaction. Are their aspects of your company that should not be up for crowd-sourcing? Lastly, Understand the difference between interaction and competitive poisoning.

Digital interaction could be used against you, can you spot the difference?

Example: All that SAAS - Converging Trends Driven By This Rapidly Evolving Model (2010)

While trends are powerful, converging trends are even more so. All year, we have focused on specific emerging trends that can each by themselves be used to create competitive advantage for businesses. That is why we take the month of November to examine the powerful combination of trends from each category that are converging to bring revolutionary change to the business environment. If change is an opportunity to dominate your market, these converging trends are your arsenal. In this article, we detail how the Software as a Service (SaaS) trend drives the converging trends of virtualization, the ad deluge, and real-time ads... and how you can use this opportunity to your advantage.

In the not so distant past, computer users grabbed the latest product disk, made sure that they had the right specifications to run the product on their machine, then set about to install and run the software. After years of this ritual many developers began to create SaaS applications to ease hard drive space and installation issues... not to mention application speed. They are designed to operate from anywhere and on any computer, and without an installation disk, which is a far cry from what software applications used to require. Now SaaS applications dominate the software industry and SaaS-sourcing is fast becoming the route to simplified operations for businesses worldwide. Not only for operational concerns but also for costs (for IT management) and ease of use. For the most part, SaaS applications even make the typical 1,000 page owner's manual seem out of place in today's world but those are not the only positive results from the SaaS revolution. Given its flexibility and costs SaaS is actually influencing other business trends as technological advances continue to skyrocket in the business space.

Perhaps the biggest trend SaaS affects is the increased presence of virtualization efforts the the business environment today, and one of those is in training. Company trainers used to operate out of the main office building, invite others to the building (if they were not already there), and conduct training sessions in a conference room. With SaaS and increased use of mobile devices, virtual training took off and now leads all other forms of training for companies. This is mainly due to the benefits of SaaS but also to increased SaaS implementation across the organization. The company saves on travel costs, time management costs, facility use, and individual software purchase and installation. Participants may log into one site and participate with other trainees as well as the instructor in those sessions... from anywhere in the world. While phone conferences worked for a while, SaaS allows a higher level of one-on-one interaction.

Similar advantages abound for employees conducting their daily activities in the name of the company. A sales force can connect to Salesforce.com at any time through their SaaS application, an analysis group can directly access statistical and database software, and inventory specialists can monitor stock in the middle of the night in case they are uneasy about product availability. Software updates? No need to worry. Every time an employee logs into the SaaS service they use the latest program without IT installing it. Operating through a virtual desktop of sorts saves companies exorbitant sums of money each year in overhead costs.

Playing off the increased use of SaaS services by virtual employees, companies have other potential tools that could benefit their bottom line and help their partners out as well. Real-time ads, placed within a website or application, dynamically change according to the piece of software used, the location of the employee, or the language that the employee uses in their communications. The same is true, and probably more relevant, for the consumer space as more and more consumers go mobile. A SaaS application in use at the local Starbucks could advertise the special for a coffee and baked good at the bottom of the application itself. In this sense SaaS provides a convenient gateway and conduit for advertising to benefit inventory control. Real-time ads are here and only going to become more prominent as companies fight for the consumer dollar.

Of course, SaaS also affected an increase in advertisements throughout the online space. As companies develop SaaS applications, there are tremendous opportunities for delivering many advertisements given the virtual warehouses of inventory space. Each application not only allows the developer to market their goods but it also provides ways for their partner companies to market their goods. This idea is something to seriously consider if you sign up for SaaS services but also if you develop them because it is an additional revenue stream for your business. However, be very careful as the advertising deluge could bring negative effects and forgetfulness if your customer becomes overwhelmed. Larger companies such as Ford and Geico can withstand the negative aspects of the advertising deluge because of their powerful brand name... many other companies cannot.

One additional aspect of the increased presence of SaaS is the relationship to mobile devices. As SaaS services become more widespread the use of mobile devices will increase and vice versa. Mobile devices and applications benefit greatly from SaaS not only due to the flexibility of applications but also to its ability to be used anywhere that has an Internet connection... the original basis of mobile. Therefore it only makes sense that these two trends operate hand-in-hand.

Over the next couple of years businesses should keep a sharp eye on SaaS services and rely less on stand-alone software products. The major reason for this is increasing smart phone adoption rates and the reliance on mobile software to run most daily computing applications. As a result companies should view SaaS applications, not only for their one-size-fits-all flexibility but also for their potential use as a gateway for other services. For example, cloud computing allowed greater SaaS usage because it minimized the need for hard drive storage. The freed space gives device manufacturers room to expand capabilities and interaction. What the world will begin to see is increased interaction to provide more personable experiences for the end user. For example, customer service agents can provide more direct and personal responses to questions. Product developers could provide an almost real-time demo of their latest offering and get feedback before even building it out fully.

What SaaS has done and will only continue to do is to pry the computing world away from a standing location and tether them to the Internet umbilical cord wirelessly. Businesses don't need to be connected to their desktop or laptop computers anymore. Does your client need to see the presentation file but does not have the right program to view it? Not any more. What we're seeing is more of the computing device as a personal attachment and SaaS encourages this view. Don't get tied down and don't lug your computer everywhere.

Of course this leads to a further deluge of ads because of this increased amount of screen time. In the next one-two years expect this to not only increase but become a bit more intrusive. Users say that they don't care much about a little ad in the corner of their application as long as the software prices are cheaper (or free). Just wait until there are splash screen ads greeting a user every time they start the program. This is coming in addition to the little ads that will show up on the top and bottom of the screen... Apple is already doing this with iAd, and is a great example of what to expect to see in the future.

To create advantage from these converging trends, consider the following. SaaS is driving a convergence of trends affecting your business. From virtualization to the ad deluge, real time ads, and other trends, SaaS is the driving force behind each. SaaS solutions exist for advantage in every part of your business. From operations to sales, marketing, human resources and more, there is nearly a sea of options. SaaS means scale, simplicity, mobility and efficiency. When you decide where to implement SaaS solutions, look for areas that will enjoy the greatest return from these benefits. Choose your SaaS solutions carefully to avoid wasted time and money. With so many SaaS solutions available, it is easy to fall for low quality solutions. Do your homework. Lastly, understand what parts of your business should NOT be SaaS-based. There are few areas indeed that should not be SaaS based but choose them carefully based on your brand, customers, security preferences and other factors.

Example: Your New Best Friend - Converging Trends Making Governments A Necessary Partner (2010)

While trends are powerful, converging trends are even more so. All year, we have focused on specific emerging trends that can each by themselves be used to create competitive advantage for businesses. That is why we take the month of November to examine the powerful combination of trends from each category that are converging to bring revolutionary change to the business environment. If change is an opportunity to dominate your market, these converging trends are your arsenal. In this article, we detail how trends are converging to make foreign government partners your new best friend in business... and how you can use this opportunity to your advantage.

Businesses across the globe seek new market opportunities daily, whether within their own borders or outside of them. This is especially true when there are down economies in their respective countries. However when it comes to realizing these opportunities, the toughest part is learning the market landscape, the regulations, the culture, or just the politics of that country at that time. The one entity that exists in every business market across the globe is government and it is this player that companies need by their side.

Governments, although in many different forms, operate every country in the world so their knowledge about the markets and the operations of that country's businesses is crucial. They can help make connections between companies, they can help network the right people into the right situations... governments are just a necessary medium for most business transactions. All company sizes can benefit from government mediation and knowledge, with some more than others. Imagine going into a country without any knowledge about its markets or customs. It would take a lot of time and effort to scope that market, find the right partners, then lay out a customer acquisition plan. They are also the keepers of the forms, enforcers of the regulations, and administrator of the business tax filings so if companies look for the quick, easy way to integrate this knowledge into their plans, they are looking at the government itself. Governments may have much of this data so going into any country without checking this first would put companies at a disadvantage.

Perhaps the biggest potential government partners are small businesses. Daniel Griswold said that, "Globalization is a fact of life in twenty-first century America," and many small companies face the "going global" question at some point in their existence. Given recent economic pressures but also opportunities small businesses blaze trails into new markets given their agility and ability to "turn on a dime." Small businesses know what they are doing when they enter overseas markets. They dominate the export markets in terms of numbers and are increasing localization efforts to "go native." Government fits into this puzzle through the availability of capital resources, such as the Import-Export Bank in the U.S., where small businesses seek loans to get their businesses off the ground overseas. Governments also act as an advisor of sorts given their vast resources of information, saving that small company a lot of money in exploration costs.

It is not just the U.S. market. Companies from across the globe explore other countries to find opportunities for their products and services. For example the Swedish-American Chambers of Commerce group acts as a mentoring and resource channel for any companies or organizations wanting to do business in either State. Companies in the UK are establishing local companies in Virginia to market and sell wine back home. Governments in the respective countries can only make this process easier for executive teams because they know the markets and the people who drive those markets. Not only do Sweden and the UK have stakes in U.S. markets but other countries from almost every continent. Again the one common entity is government who have the built-in relations and these connections should be exploited to their fullest advantage.

Of course, you know what they say... keep your friends close and your enemies closer. Governments can also be the roadblock for companies trying to create opportunities in other countries. One such roadblock instituted by many governments like China and Turkey is online regulation. Companies rely on the Internet more and more to spread their message and display their products and services... and when the internet is regulated to the point of website extinction, there are issues. Online regulation, however, only stresses the point of becoming a business partner with governments. They can help and make sure that your website it not blocked. Google made deals to operate within borders of some countries through self-regulation or policing so they are allowed to operate close to normal. It is all about working with the government and not against them. Google found out the hard way when Turkey blocked access to their sites because of their similar IP addresses to other blocked sites. You must stay in contact with governmental agencies or face the consequences.

These conversations may be easier as more and more companies go global due to the blurring lines between country and company. Examples such as the dispute between Google and China as well as the well known Microsoft and China struggle demonstrate that both parties are very much willing to discuss issues with one another... and not get any other governments involved. More interestingly still is when individual policies and agreements begin to take place between companies and governments without the aid of the company's home country. This is not too far into the future when one stops to think about it. In fact, as more companies become multi-national corporations (MNCs) there is no true "headquarters" anymore...and the executive structure will resemble more of a small country than the country they are from. In other words, we are seeing an evolution into the global MNC world where countries are either equal partners or aides to the companies themselves.

In the next one to two years pay close attention to not only the growth of global businesses, but also to the agreements and regulations that individual governments make for those MNC entities. Another evolution is that of individual small businesses joining forces to influence policies and decision-making as a group where their power and influence resembles that of the larger companies. These smaller companies will use government to get their start in the global arena but look to other smaller businesses, with similar goals, to help them the rest of the way.

It will also no longer be government to government trade as we know it... the more likely scenario is government to company to government deals. In other words, while governments are great partners for business endeavors they can also be great trading partners, taking on the role of the old commerce department. Could we see voting blocks of companies at the UN? Probably not. Companies are in a sweet spot and are on their way to becoming stronger players in the global market.

To create advantage from these converging trends, consider the following. Trends are converging to make government partners your new best friend. The blurring line between company and country, online regulation, a de-focus on the United States and increase in small businesses going global have accelerated this trend. The days when a US business was something to court globally are over. There are so many fish in the sea that your business is just not special enough to expect to be courted. Countries are just as likely as companies to make great business partners. More and more, countries are much akin to large businesses with similar concerns that you can use to help your business in their nation. Converging trends make governments your business ally or your adversary. Take your pick. Go beyond government relations to government partnerships for your global business. Form relationships that benefit you both.

Example: Individual Talent - Converging Trends Driving Your Workforce Strategies (2010)

While trends are powerful, converging trends are even more so. All year, we have focused on specific emerging trends that can each by themselves be used to create competitive advantage for businesses. That is why we take the month of November to examine the powerful combination of trends from each category that are converging to bring revolutionary change to the business environment. If change is an opportunity to dominate your market, these converging trends are your arsenal. In this article, we explore how talent and workforce trends are all driving to the idea of recognizing talent as individual... and how you can use this opportunity to your advantage.

Over the past few years businesses witnessed an evolution in the way employees want to be treated and managed. Many organizations are creating strategic talent acquisition and retention plans that center around the employee as an individual. This includes everything from training to benefits to award recognition programs. While it could be a generational trend it is nevertheless a real one and companies need to seriously track the progress if they want to attract and keep an engaged workforce. Generation X and Y employees did grow up in a culture where they were taught to be individuals and be treated as such. In order to keep these generations happy, individual attention is a must... especially with incentives and on-boarding programs.

Employees expect treatment that singles them out and does not treat them like a number. When they come in for an interview they want to be courted by the company to show that they are a hot commodity. On their first day they may enjoy a big welcome party... followed by eventual recognition awards that are specifically designed for his or her interests. It is about them. Yes, this is a general description but take a look at your workforce at this moment and decide how you make them a special part of the business... you are not going to treat them like a number and expect to keep them for any long period of time.

Starting at the beginning of employment the new employee may want to take some additional training to make them a better candidate for promotions later on in their career. Developing a program of opportunity specially designed for them is tricky if companies try to do it in-house for a number of reasons beyond the scope of this discussion. Therefore the best way is to allow outside educational opportunities such as certifications and degrees. The former includes hundreds of certifications available in nearly every industry for every conceivable skill or propensity. Employees receive the individual education that they require and the company receives a certified employee that they can show off to their clients and customers. In addition to the certifications available on the marketplace today companies can also create their own certifications for specific skills. Although these are not portable if an employee leaves, it satisfies that need for an individualized educational experience.

Once the employee is up and running in their job the next step is to offer recognition for good work. General bonus structures typically receive neutral reactions due to their almost "expected" nature every year and the pat on the back to a group of employees for a fine job just doesn't cut it anymore. Employees now look for individual recognition and rewards, including an exclusive tithe that is provided just for them and their likes. Points-based systems provide Human Resource executives the flexibility to provide customized rewards systems for individuals and, as Mike Michalowicz said, allows employers to show some level of scalability. Individuals love to compare themselves to themselves and each other so these points-based systems are ideal for individual reward satisfaction. Employees choose how they want to spend their points, whether for vacation time, a new television, or just some other perks that are not generally offered regularly. The idea is to provide employees not only gratitude for their work but also a way to show that they are not just a number in the larger company structure.

Now many workers entering the workforce over the past five to ten years are just not attached to that company structure... at all. Since they learned that they could do everything themselves many of them took the opportunity to go out on their own. This move towards freelancing is another trend affected by the individual idea. Anita Campbell suggests that, "Consultant used to be code for 'just killing time between jobs,' but now it means something more, including Entrepreneur and Small Business Owner. Much nicer titles and something that means the world to the individual worker. Since many Generation X'ers tend to remain with one company for about three years freelancing provides them an opportunity to skip job hopping and just go contract to contract. They live out the life of a project then move on before they get bored or frustrated. Generation Y'ers also benefit from this model as they provide an even more individualized look on work life, wanting to feel needed and important. If they run their own business they are the heros for saving many companies, not just one.

This is not to say that cooperation and conglomeration are dying. In fact, many freelancers form partnerships to pool their skills and resources together. Therefore they win more projects and more money because they fulfill a client's total needs. They're not stupid, they're business smart. The "I'll provide what my client needs and be that hero" attitude is great for their business and great for their clients as well.

In the next one to two years more companies will realize that they need to change their human resources philosophies if they want to keep an intact workforce. We see two directions for this trend and both are equally likely. First, successful companies will introduce individualized incentive, benefit, and work plans that speak to the employee as an individual. Recruiting materials and job ads will praise the individual and treat them like they are the most wanted worker on the planet. Incentives will follow more of the fair points-based incentive programs to eliminate any potential bias claims but that can still be tailored to the individual.

More educational opportunities will also take shape for employees as they want them but not necessarily in the traditional sense. Degrees and certifications are portable and remain the big driver of educational need, but we will see more of the individualized-focused executive teams trying to internally develop their own staff through position training. Do they want to be an executive some day in that company? Begin an educational program that provides them the skills and knowledge that moves them into the tracks for those positions. Given the generational changes occurring in employee attitudes this type of program may just be the one that makes the difference in keeping talent happy and onsite.

The other track involves the growing small business market. Freelancers and small businesses may become the majority of work styles in the world in the next two years. Again, given the individualized nature of many workers that have recently entered the workforce it makes sense that they would just work for themselves. Why not? All the freedom, all of the responsibility... it would be beneficial for their careers and lives. However the one small kink in the armor is the lack of a structure that offers praise and that is where the employee model described above may be the model that not only transforms the current make-up but also offers everything to the individual worker.

To turn these converging trends into an advantage, consider the following. Talent and workforce trends are converging on the individual. Incentives, training, promotion, mentoring, hiring and more are all becoming more focused on the worker as an individual with individual skills, motivations and goals. The most effective incentives, training and promotion are individualized. Let's face it. Everyone likes to feel special. Individualized talent strategies can scale for large companies. It does not have to be unwieldy, thanks to SaaS solutions and decentralized processes. The era of individual talent is here to stay as employee and as freelancer. These two distinct forms of worker as individual are working to spur each other. And speaking of freelancers, freelancers make individualized talent strategies easy. They are their own best retention artist and skilled in self-motivation.

Example: Driven Digital - Converging Trends Driving The Next Payment Method (2010)

While trends are powerful, converging trends are even more so. All year, we have focused on specific emerging trends that can each by themselves be used to create competitive advantage for businesses. That is why we take the month of November to examine the powerful combination of trends from each category that are converging to bring revolutionary change to the business environment. If change is an opportunity to dominate your market, these converging trends are your arsenal. In this article, we continue the theme and explore how all things digital are driving change in payment methods... and how you can use this opportunity to your advantage.

The world is quickly becoming a digital landscape due to the increasing use of technological devices. Sure, many people said this well back into the

1950s and beyond. Yet, there is something about this new digital age that is changing marketplace forces. Given the rise in mobile usage and the lack of paper transactions and interactions of any kind the world has truly entered a new realm of possibilities...especially when it comes to paying for products and services. Did you hear about the book that could help you solve a problem that you have right now but don't have the time to go to the store to get it? Just whip out your smartphone, pull down an app, find the book, and use the credit card number on file. The book is on its way. For the small business that wants to take credit cards but doesn't want the hassle of a credit card reader... just sign up for PayPal and place a button on that site. Digital technology makes it easy.

First lets focus on how the latest digital revolution has made life easier for most. PayPal and other similar online payment options rose with the increased traffic in the global marketplace. As the digital auction house eBay increased sales, PayPal allowed winning bidders the same fast and easy transactions that they enjoyed when they won their items because they didn't have to worry about how to pay someone who may live in another country. Sellers also benefitted because they didn't have to pull their product off the site unnecessarily due to nonpayment. PayPal gave small businesses the ability to accept credit cards and checks without spending a fortune on point of sale machines nor did they have to wait for a paper check in the mail. What the digital revolution in the form of Internet webpages has done is to allow the market to advance in digital payments due to technology... the technology forced a change and it was readily accepted.

This led to additional changes in the marketplace dynamics that have existed for hundreds of years. Many producers operated within a supply chain that originated in their warehouses and ended in the consumer household. Digital technology began to eliminate many distributors as producers began to go directly to the consumer. Internet technology opened the doors that only distributors opened previously and that provided more profit for producers. Customers pay less but get the same product and, possibly, a product that may have not been available before. Online shopping allows customers to choose additional colors and styles that a distributor might not have ordered because they would have had to order in bulk... and that was risky. Producers now manage the cycle and are being rewarded monetarily.

Today there is more consumer control over the market because they can choose products and services and pay for them however they like. It is all about making it easier for the customer. However it is also a necessity of operations given this changing landscape. As it becomes easier to conduct banking online, shop online, or seek services online it becomes critical to adapt payment options. If a customer is conducting business at the tips of their fingers in a split second they need to pay just as fast. As the environment changes, especially at a breakneck pace, the only survivors are those that can adapt quickly.

Of course while there are always positives, negatives emerge from this digital revolution as well. While it is difficult to comprehend how this revolution is bad for the consumer, one only needs to look toward the airline industry to see how it can be abused. Most businesses may have shied away from charging for the small cups of juice on a flight or for using the bathroom because it wouldn't make sense asking people for some spare change. However, with this new drive to a cashless society through the digital revolution, the idea of the micro-annoyance (micro-purchase) has reared its ugly head. It now feels like customers pay for everything because it is easier to charge them and ensure a new cash stream. When the customers can't pay, companies don't get the money. Now that the flood gates are open, so is the customer's wallet so that they can use the rest room during a long flight.

A cashless society then has some issues but the digital revolution continues to proceed full steam ahead. Credit cards continue to lead the way in eliminating cash but their days are numbered as well. Cashless makes it easier to conduct business online and, increasingly, in local establishments. Check the credit card pad at the cash register and just swipe your card to pay for your goods. Check your bank account online and transfer some funds over to the electric company to pay your bill. Again, it is easy and it is quickly becoming the norm. Laggards beware... digital payments are here to stay.

In the next couple of years, watch the digital revolution continue to change the way customers use money. While payment options continue to increase we see the road ahead converging on a fork. In one direction, PayPal and similar services will continue to grasp market share for online payment methods, encouraging competitors but becoming the brand name of hassle free purchases. While there will still be limitations in their current format on how they can be used, especially for local establishments, online purchases favor these services. The number of small businesses continue to grow as the economy encourages further entrepreneurial activity and they want easier payment options. Do you want to ensure prompt client payment? Given them your PayPal button. They don't have to carry cash or checks.

The other path is less clear. As digital transactions continue to increase and use different payment options, there is a need to have one type of payment method that is available all of the time. Borrowing an idea from science fiction, the alternative payment universe of the future may be one where everything is tied to you through one account. It can be your bank account, credit card, etc. The method of payment would be digital and the shop keeper would scan some kind of barcode off of you to receive payment. A more likely scenario is that our mobile phones or other similar smart devices of the future are our identity and they will carry our personal information in their memory chips. We will "bump" the cash register or send the data wirelessly to their system.

Dr. Amy Vanderbilt

To create advantage from these converging trends, consider the following. Digital payment methods are driving major precursor industry trends including micro-purchase, direct distribution, and mobile interaction. Likewise, trends are converging to drive the future of digital payment. Ease of use, security and other factors are creating market leaders and new capabilities alike. Digital payment methods will likely converge in the coming years to a small number of trusted leaders and methods. To get ahead of this trend, decide what digital payment will look like in every aspect of your business including accounts receivable and payable. Lastly, understand what markets digital payments can unlock for your business including enabling new offerings, servicing new markets and more. What can you do now that you could not do before?

Advanced Concepts

The Tea Leaves Are Hidden

It can be hard sometimes to interpret the trend data. When the data seems to make no sense, stalling out is usually to blame. When a trend stalls out, it may have to repeat one or more stages. This causes the graph to look like a fad-trend hybrid, or worse yet, it will make you think the trend is in a later stage than it really is.

The second scenario is the deadly one. Key investment and strategic decisions are made based on the trend stage. If that is read incorrectly, you are going to make the wrong move.

Example - Mobile Learning

Mobile learning is a trend in stage four with a very fad-spiked past that makes it hard to recognize. It repeated stage three after its first stage four brought it so far down in overall interest (down to stage two levels) that the first utility had been forgotten. Mobile learning was forced to repeat stage three and subsequently stage four, as a result of the significant lag.

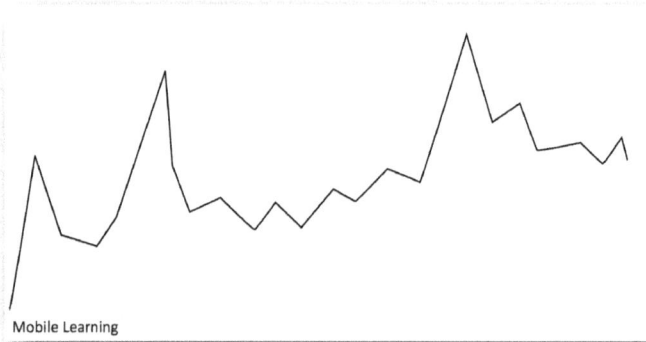

Mobile Learning

To the beginner, this graph would seem to say that mobile learning is in stage six. But the business activity in this industry does not line up with that. Take the whole industry into account to make sure you are reading the graph correctly.

A Product Ahead Of Its Time

Sometimes, a business in early startup mode, riding on a stage one trend (First Try stage), puts out a product that is ahead of its time. The executives will say, the market was not ready for it. What that really means is one of two things.

First, it may be that this product is a fine representation of the first utility for this trend, but the trend is not in that stage yet. Remember that the momentum, utility and technology all have to line up at the same time. If this is the case, you can wait it out, but you had better get your revenue elsewhere while you wait.

Secondly, and this is the hard one so listen up... your product might be one of the first tries that has simply been rejected. I'm sorry you had to hear that from me. Either way, you had better get your revenue elsewhere.

The good news is that, as most trend stages are predictable, you can make a very good guess as to when your forward thinking product might actually take off, and plan accordingly.

Trends, Trends Everywhere

We have been talking a lot about trend stages, how trends evolve, what affects their evolution, and what to do for your business as each stage. Let's turn our attention now a bit more selfishly and talk about what this means for you, your career and your own personal success. I have used trend stages throughout my career to make the right changes at the right time, and to judge where and when to go all-in with my time, effort and money. They have not let me down yet. In this topic, we explore how to apply our new understanding of trend stages to our own careers for ultimate success.

Seeing Trends Everywhere? Excellent! Welcome to My World.

I am glad to hear it! If you have not started to see trends on every street corner, it will not be long until you do. When I see a business or an industry, the first thing I see is the set of trends that drive it forward, or that will summon it's demise. I see the trends that have formed the basis of your products. Most importantly, you will start to see them too. The big moment will be when you see what comes next and can act accordingly before your competition.

Timing is everything. Can we say that enough? When to launch that product, when to innovate on the next, when to grow the business and when to shut it down; all of these decisions are better informed when you add trend stages to the mix. They are certainly not the only thing you should consider, but they are one thing that you should be sure to include.

When you return to your business, industry, team and task lists, see if you can spot the trends that form the foundation of your business. See if you can spot where they are going. Practice the skills and use that information in your strategic decision making.

Angel and Venture Investing

For angel and venture investors, trend stages are a handy map (among your other data) for when to consider getting in, and when to get out. One thing I have learned from my Venture Capital clients and friends is that getting out at the right time is almost more important than when you get into an investment. If you can get involved with a company who is riding a trend in early stage three or five, and maximize the investment until the peak of stage five, you have done about the best you can. Likewise, if you can see the end of stage five coming, and make a fast exit, you can avoid the misery of the dreaded stage six. Do not be shy to speak up in that meeting when the trends at the foundation of a potential investment are entering a pullback stage such as stages two, four or six. Understanding when NOT to invest is just as important as picking the next winner.

Product Development

In the product development world, the timing of a product launch is key. You already know that there are a multitude of factors surrounding the "right time." Is the market ready for it? (also known as momentum)... does it solve a real problem? (also known as utility)... and does it work? (also known as technology). In other words, take a close look at that product you are developing and ask yourself what the underlying trend is that you are trying to capitalize on? What stage is that trend in? Does this product represent the second utility that will shorten stage four and catapult the trend into stage five and all its wonderful associated growth? Or is the trend about to go into stage six. If your underlying trend is about to retool for longevity, your product should focus on that purpose. Don't let your product keep you in stage five blinders while the reality is stage six.

In other words, use the stage and timing of your underlying trend to help guide the type of product you put out, and when you release it.

Innovative Uses

Investing and product development, however, are not the only uses for your new understanding of trend stages. You may be asked to offer up your time and effort in any number of ways: sitting on boards of directors, advisory boards, judging competitions, the latest hobby among your friends, or that vacation home you've been thinking about. What about retirement? Which country would you like to settle down in?

When it comes to these decisions, understanding the foundational trends involved can give you a key piece of information for smarter decisions. Don't waste your time on companies that are poised for a pullback stage. Don't waste your money on houses in markets that are about to see difficult times. Focus your retirement years in countries that are about to spark growth stages.

Career Moves: Leaving Industries and Companies; and Entering New Ones

When it comes to your career, trend stages are equally applicable. Is your current organization headed for a pullback stage? Is it, in the worst of all worlds, just a fad? It pays to take a regular look at the company or organization that you work for, and the industry you work within. Chart where they are on among the seven stages. You will be in a better position to decide when to jump ship.

Likewise, when deciding which company, organization or industry to join, check those stages again. While rescuing a company from the depths of stage six can be ultimately rewarding; entering an organization and industry that is entering a growth stage is a great recipe for forwarding your career with less friction.

Conclusions

The large majority of trends evolve through seven distinct stages of growth and pullback on their way to longevity. Trends are not fads and recognizing the difference is key. More importantly, making the right move at the right trend stage is really where your company will find advantage; and your career won't suffer from that either!

Understand the trends that are present in your industry, company, and career. Track them. Understand what stage they are in now, and when and how they will go on to the next stage. Seek ways to anticipate these stages and prepare to flatten out the downturns.

This guide, is your how-to manual for doing just that. Refer to it regularly to make sure you are reading trends correctly. When in doubt, as for help. Get multiple points of view, and ultimately, act in the best interests of yourself, your business, and your industry.

Resources

Example: Under The Influence - Understanding The Stage Two Trend of Influence Marketing

Influencer marketing
http://en.wikipedia.org/wiki/Influencer_marketing

Marketing Influence: The Power of Persuasion - by Reuven Cohen - May 22, 2012
http://www.forbes.com/sites/reuvencohen/
2012/05/22/marketing-influence-the-power-of-persuasion/

Majority Of Brands Engage In Influencer Marketing: Blogs Influence On Purchase Decisions Over Social channels !! - by Shilpa Shree - February 27, 2013
http://www.dazeinfo.com/2013/02/27/blogs-influence-on-purchase-decisions-over-social-channels-report/

Social Influence Marketing is About to Change Your Business: Author of 'Return On Influence' - by: Mark W. Schaefer |Author of "Return On Influence" - Tuesday, 20 Mar 2012 http://www.cnbc.com/id/46796924/

Social_Influence_Marketing_is_About_to_Change_
Your_Business_Author_of_IsquoReturn_On_Influen
cersquo

Kill Influence Scores; Improve Influence Marketing
– by Sam Fiorella
http://spinsucks.com/social-media/kill-influence-
scores-improve-influence-marketing

Who Are the Real Online Influencers?
[INFOGRAPHIC] – By Josh Catone - Jun 13, 2012
http://mashable.com/2012/06/13/influence-
marketing-infographic/

**Example: Young and In Charge - Managing The
Stage Three Trend Of Generational Reversal**

Wise Beyond Your Years: The Challenges Of Young
Managers - By Amy MacMillan
https://www.experience.com/alumnus/article?
channel_id=career_management&source_page=ca
reer_development&article_id=article_11262863232
18

Handy tips for young leaders to take on organisational challenges - ET Bureau - Sep 27, 2012
http://articles.economictimes.indiatimes.com/2012-09-27/news/34127519_1_young-leaders-time-management-hr-director

Dear Young Manager
http://www.gradtogreat.com/tips_advice/article-an_open_letter_to_young_managers.php

How to groom Gen Y to take the company reins - December 1, 2011
http://management.fortune.cnn.com/2011/12/01/grooming-generation-y-leaders/

The six ways Generation Y will transform the workplace – By Lauren Friese and Cassandra Jowett of Talentegg - Special to The Globe and Mail - Mar. 12 2013
http://www.theglobeandmail.com/report-on-business/careers/the-future-of-work/the-six-ways-generation-y-will-transform-the-workplace/article9615027/

Unlocking the potential of Generation Y: Getting the best from young employees http://www.go2hr.ca/articles/unlocking-potential-generation-y-getting-best-young-employees

Generation Y Workplace: Millennials Who Quit Jobs To Get Ahead - 03/11/
http://management.fortune.cnn.com/2011/12/01/grooming-generation-y-leaders/

CMI_-_Generation_Y_June_2008_executive_summary - By Dr. Alison MacLeod, June 2008. Chartered Management Institute © In association with Ordnance Survey.

Example: The Smug And The Restless - Understanding Mobile Security As A Stage Three Trend

A Brief History of Mobile Time
https://www.lookout.com/resources/know-your-mobile/mobile-history

A brief history of mobile malware – by Richard Clooke - May 7, 2013
http://www.mobilecommercedaily.com/a-brief-history-of-mobile-malware

New Report Reveals History and Future of Mobile
Malware - Panda Security, the Cloud Security
Company – 2011
http://press.pandasecurity.com/usa/news/new-
report-reveals-history-and-future-of-mobile-
malware

Mobile security fails the history lesson – by Roger
A. Grimes – December 20, 2011
http://www.infoworld.com/d/security/mobile-
security-fails-the-history-lesson-182163

CNCCS – Smartphone Malware Report
The National Cyber-Security Advisory Council
(CNCCS)

HDI Executive Forum - Security Trends in a Mobile
Environment: Access in an Anytime, Anywhere
World – by Ken Huang & James Hewitt - June 22,
2011
Mobile-securitytrends-dataprotection-hdi-final-
PowerPoint

Example: Crowdfunding - Tracking This Stage Four Trend

Crowdfunding as the future of science funding? - By Anthony Salvagno in Research - May 27, 2012
http://blog.scienceexchange.com/2012/05/crowdfunding-as-the-future-of-science-funding/

The top 10 most influential crowdfunding campaigns of 2012 – By Chase Hoffberger – December 24, 2012
http://www.dailydot.com/society/top-10-kickstarter-crowdfunding-2012

Crowd funding - From Wikipedia, the free encyclopedia
http://en.wikipedia.org/wiki/Crowd_funding

A Great Way to Get Market Insight – By Jeremy Quittner, Inc.com staff - Dec 31, 2012
http://www.inc.com/magazine/201212/jeremy-quittner/a-great-way-to-get-market-insight.html?nav=featured

Unlocking the global trillion-dollar crowdfunding market – By Kevin Lawton - December 24, 2012 http://venturebeat.com/2012/12/24/crowdfunding-market

Crowdfunding Predictions for 2013 – By Ryan Caldbeck, Contributor – Dec 11, 2012
http://www.techradar.com/news/internet/crowdfunding-what-it-is-and-why-its-important-1120241

Stalled Crowdfunding Rules Leave Business Plans on Ice – By Angus Loten – December 12, 2012
http://online.wsj.com/article/SB10001424127887324339204578173731988591450.html

Building a case for crowdfunding - Business Monday – By Ina Paiva Cordle – December 30, 2012
http://www.miamiherald.com/2012/12/30/3161326/building-a-case-for-crowdfunding.html

Example: Talking Back - Understanding The Stage Four Trend Of Voice Based Systems

Will Voice Technology Change the Customer Service Game? – By Arie Goldshlager
http://www.quora.com/Customer-Service/Will-voice-technology-change-the-customer-service-game/answer/Louis-Columbus

IVR: The History And Future Of Speech Recognition – By Jay E. Coop
http://ezinearticles.com/?IVR:-The-History-And-Future-Of-Speech-Recognition&id=5771025

IVR Systems: Are They Done Yet? - By Erika Morphy, CRM Buyer - November 9, 2009
http://www.crmbuyer.com/story/68094.html

The Changing Voice of Customer Service: Does IVR work for you? – By Sumair Dutta – January 26, 2012
http://blogs.aberdeen.com/service-management/the-changing-voice-of-customer-service-does-ivr-work-for-you/

FORRESTER'S TOP 15 TRENDS FOR CUSTOMER SERVICE IN 2013 - By Kate Leggett - January 14, 2013
http://blogs.forrester.com/kate_leggett/13-01-14-forresters_top_15_trends_for_customer_service_in_2013

Why Your Customers Hate Your IVR System…and What You Can Do About It – white paper by Aspect Software - wASP_Why-Cust-Hate-IVR_Mktg-WP pdf
www.aspect.com

Example: Cyber Warfare - Anticipating Setbacks For This Stage Five Trend

A Brief Summary of Cyber Warfare – By Rob Shein, cyber security architect for HP's Security and Privacy; Professional Services division
http://www.infosectoday.com/Articles/Cyber-Warfare.htm

Cyber-warfare - Hype and fear - Dec 8th 2012 – from the print edition http://www.economist.com/news/international/21567886-america-leading-way-developing-doctrines-cyber-warfare-other-countries-

Banks brace for cyber warfare drill Quantum Dawn 2
http://www.engadget.com/2013/06/18/bank-cyberwarfare-drill-quantum-dawn-2/?utm_medium=feed&utm_source=Feed_Classic&utm_campaign=Engadget

With troops and techies, U.S. prepares for cyber warfare - By Warren Strobel and Deborah Charles - Fri Jun 7, 2013
http://www.reuters.com/article/2013/06/07/us-usa-cyberwar-idUSBRE95608D20130607

Cyber warfare 'biggest threat for businesses in 2013 - Dubai, December 9, 2012
http://www.tradearabia.com/news/REAL_226990.html

The History of Cyber Warfare – Timeline
http://online.lewisu.edu/the-history-of-cyber-warfare.asp

Silent War – By Michael Joseph Gross – July 2013

http://www.vanityfair.com/culture/2013/07/new-cyberwar-victims-american-business

Example: Data Visualization - Tracking This Stage Six Trend

Dataesthetics: The Power and Beauty of Data Visualization - By ericblue76 - October 4, 2006 http://eric-blue.com/2006/10/04/dataesthetics-the-power-and-beauty-of-data-visualization/

Empowering Business Users with Data Visualization – November 19, 2012 http://spotfire.tibco.com/blog/?p=15563

Dataesthetic Principles of Networks, Form and Design - January 1st, 2007 http://dataesthetic.org/wp/

Data Visualization Trends Favor Simple Design – October 8, 2012 http://blog.mindjet.com/2012/10/data-visualization-trends-favor-simple-design/

Data Visualization and the Art of Discovery: Beyond Number Crunching – October 10, 2012

Dr. Amy Vanderbilt

http://spotfire.tibco.com/blog/?p=14727

The Beauty of Data Visualization. Source: Ted
Talks. Speaker: David McCandless at Oxford
University – July 2010 - Duration: 21 minutes
http://www.youtube.com/watch?v=pLqjQ55tz-U

Trend five: Data visualization – By Suzie Ivelich -
December 12, 2012
http://landor.com/#!/talk/articles-publications/
articles/landor%E2%80%99s-2013-trends-
forecast-eight-hot-topics/trend-five-data-
visualization/

The Power of Data Visualization in Four Minutes -
The Joy of Stats BBC4 http://spotfire.tibco.com/
blog/?p=4807 – November 26, 2010
http://www.youtube.com/watch?
feature=player_embedded&v=jbkSRLYSojo

Data Visualization: Modern Approaches – By Vitaly
Friedman – August 2, 2007
http://www.smashingmagazine.com/2007/08/02/
data-visualization-modern-approaches/

3 Big Trends in Data Visualization – By Jorge
Garcia – December, 2011

http://blog.technologyevaluation.com/blog/
2011/12/15/3-big-trends-in-data-visualization/

New Trends in Data Visualization on the Web – by
Javier de la Torre, Sergio Alvarez (Vizzuality)
cernpdf-110119071821-phpapp01

**Example: Private Incubators - Acting on This
Stage Six Trend**

Incubators: The New Venture Capitalists? – By
Kenneth Liss – March 21, 2000 http://
hbswk.hbs.edu/item/1380.html

Pros and Cons of Incubator Funding – By David
Newton, January 24, 2005
http://www.entrepreneur.com/article/75820
Eight Reasons Startup Incubators Are Better Than
Business School – By J.J. Colao, Forbes Staff –
January 12, 2012
 http://www.forbes.com/sites/theyec/
2012/11/21/4-reasons-why-college-is-the-new-
business-incubator/

Angels, Incubators, Venture Capital and Crowdfunding… - By Mark Wallace – April 25, 2012
http://capitalistexploits.at/2012/04/on-angels-incubators-venture-capital-and-crowdfunding/

90% Of Incubators And Accelerators Will Fail And That's Just Fine For America And The World – By Peter Relan – October 14, 2012
http://techcrunch.com/2012/10/14/90-of-incubators-and-accelerators-will-fail-and-why-thats-just-fine-for-america-and-the-world/

CEO Guide to Business Incubators - By Verne Kopytoff - November 06, 2012
http://www.businessweek.com/articles/2012-11-06/the-number-and-variety-of-business-incubators-is-on-the-rise

4 Reasons Why College Is The New Business Incubator – By Young Entrepreneur Council, Contributor – November 21, 2012
http://blogs.forbes.com/theyec/

Your Capital Edge – An Entrepreneur's Finance Edge – April 24, 2012
http://www.yourcapitaledge.com/2012/04/incubators-and-accelerators-do-they-work-2/

Example: Google - Learning From This Stage Seven Supertrend

4 Keys to Google's Success
http://www.ventureblog.com/2003/05/4-keys-to-googles-success.html

The Secret to Google's Success - March 05, 2006
http://www.businessweek.com/stories/2006-03-05/the-secret-to-googles-success

Google's Quest to Build a Better Boss – By Adam Bryant - March 12, 2011
http://www.nytimes.com/2011/03/13/business/13hire.html?pagewanted=all&_r=2&

The Secret behind Google's Success – PDF
By - Abhishek Sharma - 2011

Google's Two Secrets of Success – By Panos Mourdoukoutas, Contributor – Oct 13, 2011
http://www.forbes.com/sites/panosmourdoukoutas/2011/10/13/googles-two-secrets-of-success/

Inside Google's Culture of Success and Employee Happiness - By Zach Bulygo – Feb 11, 2013 http://blog.kissmetrics.com/googles-culture-of-success/

4 Keys to Google's Success
http://www.ventureblog.com/2003/05/4-keys-to-googles-success.html

HOW GOOGLE GROWS...AND GROWS...AND GROWS – By Keith H. Hammonds – March 31, 2013
http://www.fastcompany.com/46495/how-google-growsand-growsand-grows

Our History in Depth
http://www.google.com/about/company/history/

Example: Living in the Swarm—Converging Trends Redefining the Marketplace (2011)

TrendPOV: Social Media Driving the Pace of Business - June 20, 2011
http://trendpov.com/content/operations-more/128-social-media-driving-the-pace-of-business-.html

Know Your Competition - by Rich Harshaw, CEO, Y2Marketing

http://www.businessknowhow.com/marketing/
knowcomp.htm

Negativity is contagious, study finds – by Adam
Duhachek, Shuoyang Zhang, and Shanker
Krishnan, "Anticipated Group

Interaction: Coping with Valence Asymmetries in
Attitude Shift." Journal of Consumer Research:
October 2007.
http://www.eurekalert.org/pub_releases/2007-10/
uocp-nic100407.php

Why Business Blogs Should Welcome Negative
Comments - Brad Shorr, Sept 24, 2008

TrendPOV: Market of One – Using Individualization
for Advantage - June 23, 2011
http://trendpov.com/content/operations-more/395-
market-of-one-using-individualization-for-
advantage.html

TrendPOV: Direct To Profit - Next Generation
Distribution Coming Soon To Your Industry - June
23, 2011
http://trendpov.com/content/precursors-more/365-
direct-to-profit-next-generation-distribution-
coming-soon-to-your-industry.html

TrendPOV: Double Agent – Recognizing Your Real
Competition - May 20, 2011
http://trendpov.com/content/operations-more/368-
double-agent-recognizing-your-real-
competition.html

What You Don't Know – Mining Social Media for
Competitive Intelligence - June 23, 2011
http://trendpov.com/content/operations-more/419-
what-you-dont-know-mining-social-media-for-
competitive-intelligence.html

Why User-Customized Products Are the Future of
Business (For Real This Time) - by John Paul Titlow
- April 15, 2011
http://www.readwriteweb.com/biz/2011/04/user-
customized-products-future-of-business.php

**Example: Striking the Balance - Converging
Trends Driving Global Networks with Local
Implications (2011)**

TrendPOV: Evolving Political & Economic Alliances
in the Southern Hemisphere

http://trendpov.com/content/global-more/146-
evolving-political-and-economic-alliances-in-the-
southern-hemisphere.html

Little Boxes, Glocalization, and Networked
Individualism – by Barry Wellman, Centre for Urban
& Community Studies, University of Toronto
http://www.chass.utoronto.ca/~wellman

Globalization needs an equitable balance - China
Daily - Updated: 2007-12-10
http://www.chinadaily.com.cn/opinion/2007-12/10/
content_6308821.htm

Google Books: World out of balance: navigating
global risks to seize competitive advantages - by
Paul A. Laudicina
http://books.google.com.ph/books?
id=XM3CYmJtYJcC&lpg=PA39&ots=GTksNRIWJ8
&dq=balance%20localization
%20globalization&hl=en&pg=PA40#v=onepage&q
&f=false

Globalization: The Strategy of Differences - Pankaj
Ghemawat, Published: November, 10, 2003
http://hbswk.hbs.edu/item/3773.html

TrendPOV: Accidental Isolation – Preparing to Balance Localization & Globalization http://trendpov.com/content/global-more/422-accidental-isolation-preparing-to-balance-localization-and-globalization-.html

TrendPOV: The Profit Game – Collaborating Online on Massive Global Scale http://trendpov.com/content/global-more/109-the-profit-game-collaborating-online-on-massive-global-scale-.html

TrendPOV: The Ties That Blind – Navigating Emerging Global Alliances http://trendpov.com/content/global-more/398-the-ties-that-blind-navigating-emerging-global-alliances.html

G/localization: When Global Information and Local Interaction Collide – by Danah Boyd
Citation: boyd, danah. 2006. "G/localization: When Global Information and Local Interaction Collide." O'Reilly Emerging Technology Conference, San Diego, CA. March 6.
O'Reilly Emerging Technology Conference - March 6, 2006
http://www.danah.org/papers/Etech2006.html

Example: Putting On The Breaks - How The Simplicity Backlash May Slow Efforts To Reach Your Team (2011)

No Signs of Social Media Slowdown in 2010 - by Andre Yee - January 26, 2010
http://www.ebizq.net/blogs/cloudtalk/2010/01/no_sign_of_social_media_slowdo.php

Social networking sign-up rates slow down - CBC News - February 11, 2010
http://www.cbc.ca/news/technology/story/2010/02/10/calgary-social-networking-peaks.html

It's Official: U.S. Social Networking Sites See Slow Down - by Spencer Ante

Instant Karma – Exploring Peer to Peer, Game Based & Other Innovative Motivation
http://trendpov.com/content/workforce-more/522-instant-karma-exploring-peer-to-peer-game-based-and-other-innovative-motivation.html

TrendPOV: Three Screens a Day – Reaching Employees & Customers Amid Evolving Media Consumption http://trendpov.com/content/workforce-more/478-three-screens-a-day-reaching-employees-and-customers-amid-evolving-media-consumption.html

TrendPOV: I Just Can't Tweet Another Byte – Planning for the Simplicity Backlash
http://trendpov.com/content/workforce-more/413-i-just-cant-tweet-another-byte-planning-for-the-simplicity-backlash.html

Forrester notes social media contributor slowdown - by Juan Carlos Perez - September 28, 2010
http://www.computerworld.com/s/article/9188538/Forrester_notes_social_media_contributor_slowdown

Lazy Marketers Will Be Screwed According to eMarketer Report - by Tom Johansmeyer - March 21, 2011
http://socialtimes.com/lazy-marketers-will-be-screwed-according-to-emarketer-report_b42604#more-42604

Wake-up call in social media slowdown - 2011.08.17
http://www.i-policy.org/2011/08/wake-up-call-in-social-media-slowdown.html

You'll Reach More Consumers When You Slow
Down and Think - Marketers Forced to Present
Ideas in a Nanosecond May Assume That
Customers Also Have No Time for a Quality
Message - by: Jonathan Salem Baskin - October
04, 2011
http://www.cmo.com/leadership/youll-reach-more-
consumers-when-you-slow-down-think

No signs of mobile advertising slowdown - by Staff
Reporter - 21 July 2011
http://www.vomo.co.za/no-signs-of-mobile-
advertising-slowdown/

Days of Double-Digit Growth in Social Network
Users Are Over – March 18, 2011, eMarketer
http://www.emarketer.com/
(S(21kqfrmre1yuxy55hohofeuq))/Article.aspx?
R=1008288

**Example: Rule of All - Converging Trends
Driving Your Digital Strategies (2011)**

Spotlight Ideas - 40 Key Landmarks in the History
of Digital Marketing

http://spotlightideas.co.uk/?p=4871

A Brief History of Digital Media - Russ Hopkinson - October 13th, 2009 http://threeminds.organic.com/2009/10/a_brief_history_of_digital.html

TrendPOV: Practically Online – Navigating the Evolving World of Digital Marketing http://trendpov.com/content/precursors-more/428-practically-online-navigating-the-evolving-world-of-digital-marketing-.html

TrendPOV: The Honor System – Letting Customers Name Their Own Price http://trendpov.com/content/precursors-more/503-the-honor-system-letting-customers-name-their-own-price.html

Disruptive Customer Demands - by Daniel Shefer, Director, Product Management Warp Solutions http://www.pragmaticmarketing.com/publications/topics/03/0312ds

How do you manage demand effectively? By Ken Faw – July 26, 2011 http://kenfaw.wordpress.com/2011/07/26/how-do-you-manage-demand-effectively/

How to...manage customer expectations – by Jason Compton – October, 2004
http://www.destinationcrm.com/Issue/802-October-2004.htm

Managing Customer Expectations to Improve Satisfaction - Customer Focus, Expectations and Loyalty
http://www.customerexpressions.com/cex/cexweb.nsf/(GetPages)/fb0e21c03e1a1fbb85257011006e6396

TrendPOV: Is There An App For That? – Standing Out Amid the App Deluge
http://trendpov.com/content/precursors-more/404-is-there-an-app-for-that-standing-out-amid-the-app-deluge.html

Example: All that SAAS - Converging Trends Driven By This Rapidly Evolving Model (2010)

TrendPOV: SaaS-Sourcing - Why Software As A Service Is Dominating Industries

Dr. Amy Vanderbilt

TrendPOV: Virtual Advantage - How Virtual Training, Internships, And Desktops Are Increasing ROI

TrendPOV: In The Moment - How Individual Real-Time Ads Are Becoming Reality

TrendPOV: Schizophrenic Brands - Using The Advertising Deluge To Be All Things To All Markets

Example: Your New Best Friend - Converging Trends Making Governments A Necessary Partner (2010)

TrendPOV: Grey Area - Navigating The Blurring Line Between Companies and States

TrendPOV: Small But Global - The New Face Of Global Business

TrendPOV: Freedom of Reach - Regulated Online Access And Your Global Strategy

Example: Individual Talent - Converging Trends Driving Your Workforce Strategies (2010)

TrendPOV: Skilled Proof - How Certification Programs Will Fill The Training Gap

TrendPOV: Freelance Norm - The Employee Of The Future

Example: Driven Digital - Converging Trends Driving The Next Payment Method (2010)

TrendPOV: Cashless ROI - Making The Transition Away From Cash And Checks

TrendPOV: Micro-Options or Micro-Annoyance? - The Tentative Role of Micro-Purchase

TrendPOV: Direct to Profit - Product Distribution Moving Away from Large Organizations - Music, Etc.